AQA | AS | UNIT 1

Government & Politics

People, Politics and Participat

D1334050

Paul Fairclough

Philip Allan Updates, an imprint of Hodder Education, an Hachette UK
Company, Market Place, Deddington, Oxfordshire OX15 OSE

Orders

Bookpoint Ltd, 130 Milton Park, Abingdon, Oxfordshire, OX14 4SB
tel: 01235 827720
fax: 01235 400454
e-mail: uk.orders@bookpoint.co.uk
Lines are open 9.00 a.m.–5.00 p.m., Monday to Saturday, with a 24-hour
message answering service. You can also order through the Philip Allan Updates
website: www.philipallan.co.uk

© Philip Allan Updates 2008

ISBN 978-0-340-95957-2

First printed 2008
Impression number 5 4 3
Year 2013 2012 2011 2010

This guide has been written specifically to support students preparing for
the AQA AS Government & Politics Unit 1 examination. The content has been
neither approved nor endorsed by AQA and remains the sole responsibility of
the author.

Typeset by Phoenix Photosetting, Chatham, Kent
Printed by MPG Books Ltd, Bodmin

Hachette UK's policy is to use papers that are natural, renewable and
recyclable products and made from wood grown in sustainable forests. The
logging and manufacturing processes are expected to conform to the environmental regulations of the country of origin.

AQA Unit 1

Contents

Introduction

■ ■ ■

Content Guidance

Participation and voting behaviour

Electoral systems

Political parties

Pressure groups and protest movements

■ ■ ■

Questions and Answers

Introduction

The AQA Advanced Subsidiary (AS) in Government & Politics, taught for the first time from September 2008, is a two-unit course. This guide has been written as a companion for students taking Unit 1: People, Politics and Participation. It aims to provide a clear outline of the way in which the unit is structured and examined, as well as providing students with a summary of the core content for each part of the unit. The second unit of the new AS, Governing Modern Britain, is the subject of a separate unit guide.

The specification (i.e. the syllabus) content for Unit 1 is divided into four broad areas:

(1) Participation and voting behaviour: the different ways in which people participate in a democracy; why some people choose not to participate; the main determinants of voting behaviour.

(2) Electoral systems: the roles played by elections in a democracy; the ways in which different electoral systems operate and their outcomes; different forms of democracy (representative and direct); the use of referendums in the UK, along with the arguments surrounding whether or not such devices should be used more widely.

(3) Political parties: how the main UK political parties are organised; the importance of the role played by individual party members; issues of ideology, policy and campaigning; the part played by minor political parties.

(4) Pressure groups and protest movements: the issue of pressure group classification; pressure group methods; the factors that determine a pressure group's chances of success; whether pressure groups enhance or threaten democracy.

How to use this guide

The guide is divided into three sections:

- This **Introduction** outlines the aims of the guide, provides a general overview of the unit, offers some initial thoughts regarding assessment, considers the skills required to succeed in the subject, and gives advice regarding approaches to revision and how to tackle the exam.
- The **Content Guidance** section addresses the key elements of the unit content more systematically, providing a summary of the core content, of which candidates must be able to demonstrate a good knowledge and understanding. For ease of reference, the various headings in this section mirror those in the specification.
- The **Questions and Answers** section contains a range of AS Unit 1-style questions, along with model answers of varying length and quality. The examiner comments that accompany these answers will help students understand precisely what the examiners are looking for.

The specification at a glance

Unit 1 focuses on the 'politics' of the UK as opposed to the institutions of government, which are dealt with in Unit 2. The main themes of Unit 1 are, therefore, participation and representation — how people engage with politics in the UK and how their views are heard.

The specification clearly identifies the main debates, the key concepts and the content that relate to each of the four broad areas listed on p.4. These are given in the tables below.

Participation and voting behaviour

Issues, debates and processes to be addressed	Key concepts	Content and amplification
The nature of participation in the political process	• Politics • Democracy • Pluralism • Elitism • Electorate • Apathy • Abstention	• A knowledge of different forms of political involvement: who participates and how in terms of gender, class, ethnicity, age and region • Reasons for non-participation
Participation through the ballot box	• Voting behaviour • Changing patterns of voting • Mass media	• Theories and debates concerning the long- and short-term determinants of voting behaviour, including partisan and class identification; stability and volatility; influence of issues; campaigns; party and leaders' images • By-elections

Electoral systems

Issues, debates and processes to be addressed	Key concepts	Content and amplification
The role of elections in a democracy	• Majoritarian and proportional electoral systems • Representation • Reform	• Strengths and weaknesses of first-past-the-post, single transferable vote and additional member systems • Likely effects of electoral systems on the party system • Majority and coalition governments
The nature of representation	• Direct and indirect democracy • Referendums	• Nature and use of referendums within the UK • Arguments for and against greater use of referendums within the UK

Political parties

Issues, debates and processes to be addressed	Key concepts	Content and amplification
The role of political parties in a democracy	• Political parties • Pressure groups • Party competition • 'Catch-all' parties • Ideology	• Role and function of major parties: how do parties and the party system work? • Changing ideologies: how far do political ideas shape parties? • Party structure — parties at local, national and EU levels • Programmes, policies and manifestos • Candidate and leader selection • Membership: how important are party members? • Campaigning • Minority parties

Pressure groups and protest movements

Issues, debates and processes to be addressed	Key concepts	Content and amplification
The importance of pressure groups to political communication and policy-making in a democracy	• Interest/cause • Insider/outsider • Social movements	• Factors likely to affect the political influence of groups, including membership and resources • Links with parties and government, including the EU
Pressure group behaviour	• Lobbying • Access points • Direct action • Political networks/communities • Internal democracy • Pressure group representation	• The impact of groups and movements in influencing policy and changing values • Role of the media in pressure group politics • Do pressure groups strengthen or weaken democracy? • Possibility of some citizens being excluded from pressure group politics

Revision planning

Revision is personal and the way in which you revise will be guided largely by what works for you. That said, there are a number of points you need to take on board at an early stage if you are aiming for a top grade.

First, it is important that you familiarise yourself with the main elements of the AQA specification, i.e. the Unit 1 content and the format of the examination. Specifically, you should know:

- how the unit content is divided between different sections
- precisely what you do and do not need to know in each section
- the number of questions on each paper
- how these questions relate to the sections in the unit content (e.g. one question per section of content — or a random number?)
- how much choice you will have on the Unit 1 paper (i.e. are there any compulsory questions or compulsory sections?)
- the type of questions you will face

All of this information is provided later on in this guide, though it may also be helpful for you to get hold of your own copy of the full AQA Government & Politics specification. If your teacher has not already given you this document at the start of the course your first port of call should be the AQA website (**www.aqa.org.uk**), where you will find a downloadable PDF of the full specification along with sample examination papers and other useful material. These sample papers will enable you to familiarise yourself with the range and mix of questions you are likely to face in the real examination. They will also give you the chance to see the advice and rules (or 'rubrics') that accompany the questions on the paper.

Five steps to effective revision

(1) As already mentioned, the first thing you need to do is get hold of the full AQA subject specification (syllabus), a selection of specimen papers or past papers, and any other available guidance. Make sure that all of the material you collect relates to the new 2008 specification rather than the old 'legacy' course. If in doubt, remember that the title of the old AQA Unit 1 ('GOV1 Electoral Systems and Voting Behaviour') is different from that of the new Unit 1 ('GOVP1 People, Politics and Participation'). Note that the format of the questions has changed too: the old Unit 1 papers consisted entirely of two-part questions, whereas the new Unit 1 questions are all three-part.

(2) You will need to work out a realistic revision timetable. This should incorporate all of your subjects and be broken down into focused sessions of around 40 minutes, divided by breaks. These breaks are important. If you leave no time for relaxation your revision will be less effective and you will be less likely to keep to your timetable.

(3) Using the content summary from this guide, or the specification itself, go through your folder and divide up your notes between the four broad content areas identified. It might help if you photocopy the 'paragraph' of the specification that relates to each section of the unit content, and then put these sheets on top of each pile of notes. Alternatively, you could use subject dividers labelled with the various Unit 1 section headings as a means of organising your notes. When this is done you should have several piles of notes — each one relating to a single topic — or one or more lever-arch files, divided and indexed in line with the specification content.

(4) The next task is to check your notes and make sure that you have covered all of the items on the specification. Look through each pile of notes, checking off each topic against the content summary from the specification and the core content provided in this guide. Are there big gaps? It may be that you have mislaid some notes — or that you missed some lessons and failed to catch up. It is also possible that your teacher has left out certain sections for a good reason: perhaps a lack of time if you are being entered for the Unit 1 examination in the January of year 12. Check it out. Make sure that you are not missing something vital. If you find that there are gaps, you need to work quickly. If the exam is still some way off, you may have time to reinforce any particularly thin topics by expanding the outline notes provided in the Content Guidance section, by copying up notes from friends, or by undertaking some background reading of your own. If the problem is largely down to a lack of understanding — rather than a lack of notes — you may be able to seek individual help from your teacher.

If the examination is only a few weeks away, however, something more drastic is probably called for. This guide is aimed at helping you to familiarise yourself with the scope and demands of Unit 1. Though the Content Guidance section will point you in the right direction, you will need to look elsewhere for greater depth. There are, however, a number of books on the market that provide the kind of factual summaries that can help you to cut corners if time is short, e.g. Patrick Walsh-Atkins' *AS UK Government and Politics Exam Revision Notes* (Philip Allan Updates) or Paul Fairclough's *AS & A-level Government and Politics Through Diagrams* (Oxford University Press).

(5) Look at the specification content and the available specimen papers or past papers for each module. Which questions do you feel fairly confident about tackling? Which make you want to cry or retreat to your bed with a packet of custard creams? However tempting it is to start your revision with the topics you feel happy with, it really is better to grasp the nettle and address your weaknesses first. Once you have identified these weaker areas, you need to go through making summary notes. Try — if you can — to get each small topic onto a single page. This process of summarising should eventually leave you with a much less daunting set of memory-jogging revision notes. You could also try presenting your notes in different formats. Some books, for example, present the information in the form of diagrams. You could try turning these diagrams into prose or into bullet points. Equally, try turning some of your own handwritten notes into diagrams. You will find that the very process of reformatting your notes in this way reinforces learning and develops a greater understanding of the material.

Five points to avoid

(1) Leaving your revision until it is too late. Though last-minute revision may have served you well at GCSE, students who adopt this approach at AS and A-level rarely come away with the kinds of grades of which they are capable. The depth of knowledge and understanding required at this level makes it difficult to use quick fixes.

(2) Staying at home when you should be attending in-school revision sessions. Though you may feel that you can do a better job yourself, the vast majority of students who adopt this approach do not achieve their potential. However pointless the school revision lessons may seem to you, they are probably helping you more than you realise.

(3) Revising for hours without a break or working for whole days on a single subject. A series of 40-minute sessions interspersed with 15-minute breaks can lead to more productive work. It is good to build some daily variety into your revision programme, by mixing and matching different subjects.

(4) Question spotting. Although it is recommended that you look at the kinds of questions that have turned up in the past, question spotting (i.e. trying to guess what the examiners will put on the exam paper) is a dangerous game. Even if your 'banker' topic does turn up, there is no guarantee that it is going to be phrased in such a way that you will want to tackle it.

(5) Leaving out major topics from your revision. This can be disastrous. I regularly mark examination scripts where candidates who are obviously able score a high A grade on one question and yet barely scrape a C grade on the other. The free choice of questions available in Unit 1 means that you will never be forced to answer a question, but failing to revise one or more of the four sections of unit content will seriously reduce your options if something really nasty should appear on one of your preferred topics. It will also limit your overall ('synoptic') under-standing of the subject, as is made clear in the specification:

Students must study all four sections of this unit. There are no optional topics within this unit. This unit will form the basis for later study and students will need to cover all topics as they may need to make reference to them in synoptic questions at A2.

Examinable skills

The Qualifications and Curriculum Authority (QCA) have identified the three assess-ment objectives (AOs) common to all three main Government & Politics specifications. At AS (i.e. Units 1 and 2), the assessment is weighted more towards AO1 (knowledge and understanding), whereas at A2 (i.e. Units 3 and 4), the emphasis shifts slightly, with 45% weighted for AO1 and 35% for AO2 (analysis and evaluation). Though this shift clearly reflects the greater emphasis on analysis and evaluation required at A2, you will obviously need to do more at AS than simply demonstrate knowledge.

Assessment objectives		AS weighting
AO1	Demonstrate knowledge and understanding of relevant institutions, processes, political concepts, theories and debates.	50%
AO2	Analyse and evaluate political information, arguments and explanations, and identify parallels, connections, similarities and differences between aspects of the political systems studied.	30%
AO3	Construct and communicate coherent arguments making use of a range of appropriate political vocabulary.	20%

Your AQA Unit 1 answers will be marked according to these assessment objectives. Examiners will not simply give you a mark out of 40 for each of the questions you tackle; marks will be available for each assessment objective, and the total mark for the question will therefore be arrived at by totalling the marks awarded for knowledge and understanding (AO1), analysis and evaluation (AO2) and communication (AO3) on each sub-question.

As we will see in the Questions and Answers section of this guide, there are four key elements to achieving a good mark when answering these questions:

(1) Take time to identify what the question is getting at — i.e. what you are being asked to do. Look for command words (e.g. discuss, analyse, evaluate, identify) and make sure that you do what is being asked of you.

(2) Try to write in an analytical (i.e. argument-led) style as opposed to simply describing. The latter may be rewarded on AO1, but you are unlikely to pick up many marks on AO2.

(3) Strike the right balance between theory and supporting examples. Ideally, each separate argument/point should be developed in a single paragraph and each point that you make should be supported by at least one example.

(4) Try to use appropriate political vocabulary. This will help you to score more highly on AO3.

As well as providing the outline assessment objectives for all A-level Politics specifications, the QCA has also provided performance descriptors for answers at the A/B grade boundary and the E/U grade boundary. These descriptors (see p. 11) are rather generic, but they do give you a good idea of what is required to achieve one of the top two grades.

Performance descriptors at AS

Grade	AO1	AO2	AO3
A/B boundary	Candidates characteristically: **(a)** demonstrate full and accurate knowledge of political institutions and processes and a sound understanding of political concepts, theories and debates **(b)** produce answers that deploy relevant knowledge to answer the question **(c)** demonstrate clear contextual awareness **(d)** use relevant evidence and, where appropriate, contemporary examples to illustrate points made	Candidates characteristically: **(a)** provide analyses that display a sound awareness of differing viewpoints and a clear recognition of issues **(b)** evaluate political institutions, processes and behaviour, applying appropriate concepts and theories **(c)** make valid comparisons	Candidates characteristically: **(a)** construct and communicate clear, structured and sustained arguments and explanations **(b)** use accurate political vocabulary
E/U boundary	Candidates characteristically: **(a)** demonstrate a basic knowledge of political institutions and processes and begin to show some understanding of political concepts, theories and debates **(b)** make a limited attempt at answering the question **(c)** produce at least one piece of relevant evidence, which may be drawn from source material provided	Candidates characteristically: **(a)** show some basic awareness of differing viewpoints **(b)** attempt simple evaluation of political institutions, processes and behaviour **(c)** make simple comparisons	Candidates characteristically: **(a)** attempt to communicate and develop an argument or explanation **(b)** use basic political vocabulary

On the examination day

Below are a few general points about how to maximise your chances in examinations once the revision is complete and the big day has finally arrived.

(1) Ensure that you know which topics/units are being examined on which day. This might sound obvious but it is not uncommon for candidates to miss examinations inadvertently, or to turn up having revised Latin Unit 2 only to find that they are in fact due to sit Politics Unit 1. It may be that you have an examination clash involving two or more subjects. If this is the case, make sure that you know which unit(s) you will be doing in the morning and which you will be sitting in the afternoon. It is your responsibility to make sure that you know which exam is on which day and whether exams are in the morning or afternoon. Even if you have revised for both subjects that are being examined on the same day, it can be unsettling suddenly to discover that you are tackling them in a different order from that which you had expected. These kinds of mistakes can cost grades.

(2) Make sure that you arrive in good time for the examination. If you arrive at the last minute, or even late, you will probably not be in the best frame of mind to tackle the examination paper. Arriving far too early can be just as bad if you are nervous by nature, as you may well manage to get yourself into a state before you even enter the examination room.

(3) Make sure that you arrive properly equipped. You should know what you need for the examination. Do not turn up without a pencil if you have spent your whole revision programme planning essays in pencil before you start. More importantly, think carefully about what pen you are going to use. Examiners frequently complain about the problems they have reading scripts written in scratchy and/or faint biro. It makes far more sense to use a black roller ball pen, a black gel pen or a black ink pen in examinations. Why lose valuable marks simply because your words of wisdom cannot be read?

(4) Timing is crucial. You must make a mental note of the total time allowed for the examination and the amount of time you have available to complete each question. It can be helpful to make a note of the times at which you should be beginning each question or sub-question at the start of the examination. This will help you to make sure that you do not fall behind schedule. Remember, the number of extra marks that you will gain by spending a further 10 minutes on a question that you have already answered well will not make up for the marks you will lose as a result of only having 15 minutes left to answer the last question. Be strict with yourself!

(5) Think carefully before you commit pen to paper. Although it can be tempting to start writing as soon as you open the question booklet, particularly if everyone else is scribbling away, it is far better to have a good look at all of the questions first to make sure that you haven't missed anything. It might be that the question on voting behaviour is there, after all, but it is just worded in a less obvious way. It would be a shame to miss your 'banker' topic as a result of your eagerness to start writing straightaway.

(6) Make sure that you do what is asked of you rather than simply writing what you want to write. If the question says 'explain' do not simply 'describe'. If it asks you to consider a particular period (e.g. the 1990s) then focus on that period rather than reeling off all of your examples from the 1960s.

(7) Strike the right balance between political theory and supporting examples. Answers that are overly theoretical, or those that simply describe recent events without any attempt to bring in theory, are likely to fail. Anyone can do the latter if they watch the news. You have been studying politics for at least a year and you should, therefore, be able to bring political theory into your evaluation of events, as well as putting those events into their historical context.

About the exam

Scheme of assessment

The switch from the old three-unit AS to the new two-unit model was accompanied by a 50% increase in the length of each AS unit examination — from 1 hour up to 1½ hours. Each of the two AS units (GOVP1 and GOVP2) now account for 50% of the total AS mark (25% of the overall A-level mark).

Exam format

AQA UNIT 1 (GOVP1): People, Politics and Participation

Exam type	Written
Duration	1½ hours
Question choice	Candidates must answer any two questions from a choice of four
Question format	Each question consists of three parts (a, b and c) worth 5, 10 and 25 marks respectively. Each question is accompanied by a short piece of source material
Question focus	Each of the four questions on the exam paper will relate to one of the four sections of the specification content for the unit
Total marks available	80
Overall weighting	50% of the total AS marks (25% of the total A-level marks)

Timing

With each examination paper carrying a maximum of 80 marks and lasting 90 minutes, it is far easier to decide how much time to spend on each question than was once the case. Essentially, you should spend around 5 minutes on each part (a) question, 10 minutes on the part (b)s and around 25–30 minutes on the longer part (c) mini-essays.

Tackling the exam

Before you start writing

First, remember to scan through the whole paper before you start writing your first answer. It would be crazy to finish question 1 and get halfway through question 2 before you realised that your favourite topics had turned up on questions 3 and 4.

Second, make sure that you take time to read through all three parts of your chosen question before you commit yourself to taking it on. It is all too easy to waste time including irrelevant material in the 5-mark part (a) question, only to find that you are then required to write out the same material in parts (b) or (c). In an examination where every second is vital, you simply cannot afford to squander 2 or 3 minutes in this way.

The 5-mark part (a) questions

These questions ask you to explain a term or phrase used in the extract provided.

How to write an A-grade answer
- The first thing you need to do is provide a concise and unambiguous definition.
- Remember that this term is likely to be part of the vocabulary of politics. You should therefore be defining the term as it is used in the study of the subject, rather than just using a generic dictionary definition.
- Once you have provided your definition, you should use the material in the extract and/or your knowledge to explain the term more fully.
- Try to make sure that you provide at least one example in support of your answer.
- Remember, all of the marks on this question are awarded for AO1 (knowledge and understanding), so there is no need to give detailed analysis or evaluation in your answer.

The 10-mark part (b) questions

Part (b) questions instruct you to use both the extract and your own knowledge to examine briefly a particular issue or argument. Remember that 'knowledge' can include an awareness of relevant theories, concepts and political models, as well as factual examples.

How to write an A-grade answer
- Make sure that you define any relevant terms early in your answer.
- Remember, it is far better to identify three or four main points and tackle them well than to deal with six or seven points in a superficial fashion.
- Provide a clear focus on the precise terms of the question set, right from the start, perhaps by making explicit reference to words or phrases in the question itself.
- Make sure that you remember and make reference to any debates or controversies surrounding the topic under discussion.

- Do not forget that on these questions the marks for AO2 (analysis and evaluation) are equal to those for AO1 (knowledge and understanding).

The 25-mark part (c) questions

Part (c) questions are, in effect, mini-essays. The question will normally offer a short quotation (often a sentence outlining a particular point of view) followed by any one of a number of command words or instructions, e.g. 'discuss', 'assess the accuracy of this view', 'to what extent would you agree with this view?'.

How to write an A-grade answer

- As with the part (b) questions, it is important that you define any key terms early on and focus on the precise terms of the question posed from the outset. Quoting phrases or key words from the title periodically throughout your answer can be a good way of demonstrating an explicit focus.
- Make sure that you impose a clear analytical structure on your answer from the outset. Part (c) mini-essays are likely to be anywhere between one-and-a-half to two-and-a-half sides long. Adopt a structure that addresses around four factors, with one developed paragraph per factor. At the end of each paragraph ask yourself whether you have related it back to the question. If not, add a linking phrase or sentence to the end of the section.
- Try to provide some balance in your answer, i.e. avoid presenting an answer that is totally one-sided. Try to be objective, as opposed to subjective, even if you feel strongly about the issues under debate.
- Do all that you can to integrate political theory alongside supporting examples. Favouring one at the expense of the other will make it far harder for you to reach the higher levels on the mark scheme.
- Remember that on these longer questions, 6 of the 25 marks available are awarded for communication. This is not just about demonstrating sound spelling, punctuation and grammar; you also need to make use of subject-specific vocabulary.

Content Guidance

This section of the guide aims to address the key areas of content, the central issues and the main arguments pertinent to each of the four AQA Unit 1 sections: Participation and voting behaviour; Electoral systems; Political parties; and Pressure groups and protest movements.

While it is clearly not possible to answer every conceivable question here, this Content Guidance provides thorough yet concise coverage of all the core topics. This material is best used as the basis for further study.

Participation and voting behaviour

The nature of participation in the political process

What is politics?

The political process is the process by which conflicts are resolved. Within any society conflict will arise as a result of:

(1) **Scarcity of resources:** where certain goods are in short supply, conflict will result over the distribution of the available resources.

(2) **Ideological differences:** individuals might take radically different views of the way in which society should be organised.

(3) **Differences in approach:** individuals may share an ideology but have different approaches to achieving their common goals.

(4) **Divisions of labour and power:** individuals might be unhappy about their own position within society. Conflict might result from their desire to challenge the status quo.

The study of politics must, therefore, involve a focus on conflict resolution and, in particular, an examination of the way in which power is divided up between individuals, between individuals and the state, and between the different institutions that make up the state. In theory, all laws should serve to discourage behaviour that is detrimental to the common good and encourage that which is beneficial.

What is democracy?

The term democracy comes from the Greek *demokratia* — a union of *demos* (meaning 'the people') and *kratos* (meaning 'power'). Literally, therefore, democracy is 'rule by the people' or 'people power'. Some argue that the word *demos* could just as easily be defined as 'the mob'. This would leave democracy as 'mob rule' or 'mobocracy'. Writers such as John Kingdom see a natural progression from the 'pure form' of democracy to the corrupt form of mob rule.

Within this broad definition a distinction is commonly drawn between representative democracy and what is known as direct democracy. The distinction between these two forms is dealt with on p. 44.

What do we mean by 'pluralist democracy'?

Pluralism is a system of government that encourages participation and allows for free and fair competition between competing interests.

In a pluralist democracy:
- there will be a diverse range of competing interests
- there will be numerous access points — points of leverage where pressure groups can exert influence
- no single group will be able to exclude any other from the political process

It is commonly argued that the UK is a pluralist democracy. Some people, however, maintain that the UK system of government is in fact dominated by **elites**: that members of a particular social class, those of a particular educational background, or those who move in particular social circles (virtuous circles) dominate the higher levels of government, industry and the media.

People who share the view that elitism rather than pluralism is the defining characteristic of the UK system would maintain that the democratic process is more for show than for bringing about substantive changes. This is because the governing elite will always work to maintain its own interests. In this way, New Labour's rebranding under Tony Blair after 1994 might have had the effect of making the party more acceptable to the dominant elite and, therefore, worthy of support in the face of a divided and unstable Conservative Party. Writers such as C. Wright-Mills, in his book *The Power Elite*, have made similar criticisms of the US system of government.

Power and authority

Absolute power is the ability to do something — to make something happen. In reality, this form of power exists only rarely, as even the ultimate threat — death — will not force every individual to act as required.

With absolute power unachievable, we often use the term 'power' to refer to the ability to make things happen because others:
- are persuaded of the merits of a given course of action (**persuasive power**)
- accept an individual's right to make decisions (**legitimate power**)
- are forced by means of laws and penalties (**coercive power**)

Authority is the right to make something happen — the right to take a particular course of action. It can involve the legitimate exercise of power. Power and authority may be held independently of one another:
- A bomb-wielding terrorist may have power without authority.
- A teacher might have authority without genuine power.
- An officer in a tactical firearms unit may have power and authority.

In the same way that efforts to define power often result in prefacing the term with other words, the German sociologist Max Weber (1864–1920) identified three sources of legitimate authority: **traditional authority** (based on established traditions and customs), **charismatic authority** (based on the abilities and personalities of individual leaders), and **legal-rational authority** (granted as a result of a formal process such as an election).

The context of political participation

The nature of political participation within a given state will be influenced, in part, by the prevailing political culture. According to Lynton Robins, political culture consists of 'the opinions, attitudes and beliefs which shape political behaviour. A country's political culture consists of the whole citizenry's collective attitudes to the political system and their role in it.'

In the 1950s and 1960s, UK political culture was said to be characterised by homogeneity, consensus and deference.

Homogeneity
This is the view that people within a country share certain key values — a sense of togetherness which transcends that which divides them. Developments such as the expansion of immigration since the 1960s, the rise of Scottish and Welsh nationalism, and the decline of the Church of England have created a situation in which the UK is often said to be characterised more by **multiculturalism** than by homogeneity.

Consensus
This is where UK citizens accept the basic 'rules of the game'. These rules include the need for tolerance and pragmatism, for peaceful negotiation and compromise. The postwar consensus ended with the rise of politicians such as Margaret Thatcher in the 1970s. In recent years this decline in consensus has also been reflected in the proliferation of single-issue campaigns, the rise of direct action, and increased support for nationalist parties.

Deference
This is the view that people defer to an elite that is seen as 'born to rule' — a natural willingness to accept an ingrained class-based inequality, or hierarchy. The power of the ruling elite was often perpetuated by the veil of secrecy and mystery that surrounded it. In recent times the development of a modern, less deferential media has done much to demystify such individuals and institutions. Unthinking deference to such elite figures has, as a result, declined significantly.

Different forms of participation

Electoral participation
Those who are both eligible and registered to vote in a given election are referred to collectively as the **electorate**. Under the Representation of the People Act (1969) the franchise (the right to vote) was extended to citizens aged 18 or over. The effect of this Act and other changes dating back to the Great Reform Act (1832) was to significantly increase the number of individuals eligible to vote.

- In 1831, only 5% of over-18s were able to vote. This represented 450,000 individuals from a population of around 25 million.
- By 1969, 99% of adults had the vote. This was round 40 million individuals from a population of 58 million.

In the UK voters are legally required to register to vote. In 2004, 95% of the voting age population (VAP) was registered to vote. It is important to remember, however, that British citizens living abroad also retain the right to vote. In addition, not all of the UK VAP is entitled to vote. You cannot vote in UK parliamentary elections if you are:

- a European Union citizen from an EU country other than Britain or Ireland. (Note, however, that European citizens can vote in European Parliament elections and local elections in any EU country in which they are living)
- a member of the House of Lords
- a convicted criminal who is in prison
- convicted of a corrupt or illegal electoral practice
- suffering from severe mental illness

Turnout and abstention

One of the most obvious ways in which an individual can participate within a political system is to vote. Levels of turnout are, therefore, an important measure of political participation.

General election turnout (1945–2005)

Year	%	Year	%	Year	%	Year	%
1945	72.8	1959	78.7	1974 (Feb)	78.8	1987	75.3
1950	83.9	1964	77.1	1974 (Oct)	72.8	1992	77.7
1951	82.6	1966	75.8	1979	76.0	1997	71.4
1955	76.8	1970	72.0	1983	72.7	2001	59.4
						2005	61.5

Low turnout is a problem because it brings into question the government's legitimacy and the strength of its electoral mandate. In 2005, for example, the Labour Party secured a Commons majority of 65 with the support of only 35.2% of the 61.5% of eligible voters who turned out to vote. This is equivalent to 21.6% of the electorate. When considering turnout one should, however, remember three points.

First, the national turnout figure masks massive regional variations. In the 2001 general election, for example, independent Dr Richard Taylor won on a 75% turnout in Wyre Forest, despite a record low turnout of only 59% nationwide. In a similar vein, though the national turnout in 2005 was 61.5%, there was a significant gulf between the highest constituency turnout (80.2% in West Tyrone) and the lowest (41.4% in Liverpool Riverside). This variation is referred to as **differential turnout**.

A number of factors might account for differential turnout:

- how marginal an individual seat or election is (is there a chance to make a real change?)
- the electoral system in operation (do people think their vote will count?)
- local or national issues and/or controversies — the intensity of the campaign
- media attention (greater or lesser media activity in one constituency or in a given election may affect turnout)

Following this logic, the 59.4% turnout in the 2001 general election may have resulted from the sense that Labour was 'bound to win', from a lacklustre campaign, or from the lack of a real choice between the major parties.

Second, turnout varies considerably according to variables such as age, gender, social class and ethnicity. Older voters, women, those in higher social classes and Caucasian voters are statistically more likely to turn out. For example in 2005, 89% of those who were over 75 cast a ballot, whereas only 45% of 18–24-year-olds did so.

Third, turnout varies significantly between different types of elections, e.g. local, general, EU and by-elections.

Why is turnout often so low?
(1) **Intelligent voters:** voters are more likely to turn out to vote when they can see that the resulting institutions are important.
(2) **Disaffected or apathetic voters:** an increasing number of voters are coming to the conclusion that elections don't matter, as 'all parties are the same'. As a result they simply cannot be bothered to vote.
(3) **Media-driven voters:** some people only vote when the media bring the elections to their attention, abstaining in low profile elections.

Some people have suggested that a proportion of those who abstain do so because they are happy with the status quo and do not, therefore, feel the need to cast a ballot (this is sometimes referred to as 'hapathy'). Though this might appear to be a somewhat perverse view, it is not totally at odds with research on voting behaviour conducted for the Electoral Commission in 2005, where 29% of those who described themselves as 'satisfied with democracy' did not vote in the 2005 general election, and 59% who were 'dissatisfied with democracy' still turned out.

Non-electoral participation
Studies of political participation often focus on electoral participation defined in narrow terms, i.e. turnout. If we adopt a more inclusive definition of electoral participation we might include activities such as:

- canvassing and leafleting
- organising election events and fundraising activities
- staffing campaign offices

It is also important to remember that there are many forms of non-electoral participation, not least:

- individually writing to one's MP or councillor

- having an ongoing membership of and/or involvement with a political party
- engaging in pressure group activity

Recent years have witnessed a move away from traditional forms of participation (e.g. voting, party membership), through membership of mainstream pressure groups, to involvement in protest movements, consumer campaigns and direct action.

Though this process was already well underway by 2000 (see the table below), it has gathered pace since, with low turnouts in the 2001 and 2005 general elections and the rise of protest politics, such as over fuel prices, fox-hunting, globalisation and Iraq.

Changes in participation (%), 1984–2000

Type of activity	1984	2000
Voted in a general election	83	72
Signed a petition	63	42
Contacted a public official	25	25
Boycotted products for ethical reasons	4	31
Contacted the media	4	9
Attended a political meeting	9	6
Attended a demonstration	5	5
Attended an illegal protest	1	2

Source: P. Whiteley, 'The state of participation in Britain', *Politics Review*, Vol. 16, No. 1.

The sharp decline in individual party membership in the last 30 years has been contrasted with the steep rise in pressure group membership. In 2004, the Royal Society for the Protection of Birds (RSPB) had more members than the three main UK political parties combined.

Royal Society for the Protection of Birds

- over 1 million members
- a staff of over 1,300 people and over 8,800 volunteers
- an income of over £50 million per year
- a UK headquarters, three national offices and nine regional offices
- a network of 175 local groups and more than 110 youth groups

Individual party membership, 1950–2007

Party	1950	1979	2007
Conservative Party	c.2.8m	c.1.2m	c.300,000
Labour Party	c.1.5m	c.700,000	c.200,000
Liberal Democrats	–	–	c.70,000

Thus, as Noreena Hertz remarked in the *Independent* following the record low turnout in 2001: 'It's not about apathy...while voting is waning, other forms of political expression are on the rise.'

Who participates and how?

Gender and voting

In 1967, Pulzer noted that 'there is overwhelming evidence that women are more conservatively inclined than men.' Why was this? Some argued that the traditional position of women in the home made them more in tune with the Conservative Party's emphasis on family and law and order, whereas unionised men were more likely to vote with their class party.

The closing of the gender gap since 1979 may, in part, be due to changes in society, e.g. the changing roles of women or the declining influence of unionised labour. New Labour's efforts to court the female vote may also have played a part, e.g. more women-friendly policies, the creation of a minister for women, and the use of all-women shortlists in many safe Labour seats. Such changes may in fact have had the effect of reversing the traditional imbalance. In 2005 women actually favoured Labour over the Conservatives (38%:32%), whereas the male vote was split evenly (34%:34%).

Class and voting

What is class?

In general terms a social class is a group of individuals who share a common position within society. Market researchers tend to divide people up into six socioeconomic classes:

A	higher professional, managerial, administrative
B	intermediate professional, managerial, administrative
C1	supervisory, clerical, other non-manual
C2	skilled manual
D	semi-skilled and unskilled manual
E	residual, casual workers, people reliant on state benefits

Links to voting behaviour?

In the 1960s Pulzer concluded that 'class is the basis of British party politics; all else is embellishment and detail.' The working class voted Labour and the middle classes were expected to vote Conservative. In the 1950s and 1960s this might well have been the case. This was a period of high **partisan alignment** and **class alignment**. That is to say, people were attached to one party for which they tended to vote, and their chosen party was often said to be the party of their class.

The relationship between class and voting has, however, been undermined by broader societal changes that have taken place since Pulzer made his comments. The decline in traditional heavy and manufacturing industries and the rise of the service sector had a massive impact on employment. Between 1955 and 1996 employment in the service sector increased from 36% to almost 76% of all workers, while manufacturing employment fell from 43% to 18%. By 1996 only 0.9% worked in heavy industry and many nationalised industries (e.g. steel, gas, water, British Telecom) had been transferred to the private sector. At the same time, more women came into the workforce, there was an increase in part-time work and the number of people who were self-employed increased by 75% between 1979 and 1990.

The old industries were often male dominated, labour intensive and heavily unionised. The Labour Party's links with the trade unions meant that they often did well in areas dependent on this kind of industry. With the decline of such industries and the emergence of a less unionised service sector, the Labour Party's core support became more difficult to identify. It was against this background that Ivor Crewe talked about the decline of the 'old working class' and the rise of the 'new working class'. The privatisation process and the introduction of competition to many of these areas (profit sharing, performance-related pay etc.) was said to make people more individualistic and less in tune with the kind of social engineering favoured by Labour.

The extension of share ownership was one factor that made some in the working classes feel more middle class, which was part of a process of **embourgeoisement** (where working-class people feel more middle class and therefore vote for 'the party of the middle classes'). Changes in the pattern of home ownership also had the effect of undermining traditional class ties. The Housing Act 1980 gave long-term council house tenants the 'right to buy' their homes at discounts of 50–70% of the market value. When the majority of working-class people lived in council houses they had an obvious link with and reliance on the state, e.g. it was the council that repaired their house. By allowing these tenants to buy their own houses, the Conservative administrations of the 1980s turned them into 'owner-occupiers', a group who would be far more likely to identify with the Conservative Party at general elections.

Class and voting since 1979

The cumulative effect of these changes is that since Pulzer's time many commentators have charted what they have described as a process of **class de-alignment**.

The Alford Index (calculated by subtracting the percentage of non-manual voters voting Labour from the percentage of manual voters voting Labour) went down from 42% in 1964 to only 22% in 1997. Margaret Thatcher attracted C2 voters, the 'working-class Tories', and Labour under Tony Blair broadened its appeal to include many AB voters. For David Denver, the 1997 election with its 10+ swing underlined the validity of the de-alignment thesis. This is because long-term factors such as social class should remain relatively constant over time, and a decline in the influence of such factors should, therefore, result in greater volatility and greater swings.

The 2005 general election witnessed both Labour and the Conservatives losing support among AB voters to the Liberal Democrats. The election also saw the Conservatives regain support among the C2s, the 'working-class Tories' who had backed the party in the 1980s. However, although the strong correlation that once existed between social class and voting has clearly declined over time, it remains an important influence.

% votes by class, 2005 (2001)

Party	AB	C1	C2	DE
Labour	28 (33)	32 (40)	40 (47)	48 (49)
Conservative	37 (40)	36 (33)	33 (29)	25 (28)
Lib Dem	29 (21)	23 (21)	19 (17)	18 (17)
Other	6	9	8	9

Ethnicity and voting

In 1996 the ethnic minority population of Great Britain was said to number around 3.3 million, or 6% of the population. By the time of the 2001 census this figure had reached 4.6 million (8%).

Though only 8% of voters come from an ethnic minority, these groups are often concentrated in urban areas, and so can affect the outcome of individual constituency contests. Even in the early 1990s, Bill Coxall and Lynton Robins estimated that there were around 49 seats where the margin of victory was smaller than the number of ethnic minority voters in their constituency. Traditionally, the majority of ethnic minority voters have tended to support the Labour Party, whether due to tradition, the party's policies or Labour's broader support for the deprived, urban communities in which ethnic minority voters are disproportionately likely to live.

That said, Labour is not guaranteed the votes of such groups. The party's support for military intervention in Iraq, for example, had a significant impact on its popularity in constituencies with high Muslim populations (see the table on p. 28). This was most notable in Bethnal Green and Bow, where the incumbent Labour MP Oona King lost her seat to the former Labour MP and Respect candidate George Galloway.

2005 general election results in British constituencies with large Muslim populations (based on % of population of Muslim religion from 2001 census)

| | % Muslim | Rank | Change in % share 2001–05 (% points) | | |
			Con	Lab	LD
Birmingham, Sparbrook and Small Heath	48.8	1	–1.7	–21.4	+7.0
Bethnal Green and Bow	39.2	2	–10.1	–16.4	–4.3
Bradford West	37.6	3	–5.4	–7.9	+11.9
East Ham	29.7	4	–3.5	–19.2	+3.9
Birmingham, Ladywood	29.5	5	–0.7	–17.0	+23.3
Blackburn	25.7	6	–8.3	–12.1	+12.5
Poplar and Canning Town	25.4	7	+2.0	–21.1	+2.8
West Ham	23.6	8	–4.7	–18.7	+3.5
Bradford North	20.6	9	–7.9	–7.2	+12.5
Ilford South	19.6	10	+1.5	–10.8	+9.3

Source: General Election 2005 House of Commons Research Paper 05/33, May 17, 2005.

Age and voting

It is generally accepted that older voters are more likely to vote Conservative, whereas younger voters favour Labour. This is one of the reasons why it was argued that lowering the voting age from 21 to 18 in 1969 would favour more radical parties.

This still holds true to a large degree, as witnessed by voting behaviour in the 2005 general election (see the table below), although Labour's support for the war in Iraq and its introduction of top-up fees contributed to a significant drop in support for the party among younger voters.

| Party | Age | | |
	18–34	35–54	55+
Labour	37	41	32
Conservative	28	29	41
Liberal Democrat	27	22	40

Some attribute such age-related voting patterns to the fit between the kinds of policies traditionally favoured by the Conservative Party (e.g. pro-family, law and order) and older voters, whereas others argue that people simply become more conservative (i.e. less radical) in outlook as they get older. Some maintain that the traditional correlation between age and voting behaviour reflects the relative strengths of the parties when those who are now older were young. This would mean that future generations of old voters may support Labour over the Conservatives.

The '**grey vote**', as it is known, is likely to become even more significant in light of the UK's ageing population demographic.

Region and voting

During the 1980s political scientists focused on the apparently growing economic division between the prosperous south and the northern parts of the country. This was known as the '**North–South divide**'.

At that time, many northern-based primary industries (e.g. mining) and manufacturing industries (e.g. textiles) were in decline, whereas the service and financial sectors — often based in the home counties — were booming. By 1994 the average income per head of those in the north was only 89% of the average for the UK as a whole, while unemployment in the region was 10.8 % compared to the average UK figure of 8.6%. There were also marked differences in health and life expectancy between those living in the north and those in the south.

Because this North–South divide reflected longstanding socioeconomic cleavages, it was also reflected in voting behaviour. Labour was strong in the north, Scotland and Wales, whereas the Conservatives fared better in the southeast (the home counties). For instance, in 1997 the Labour Party achieved 51.8% of the votes (46 seats) in the north compared with the Conservatives' 27.9% (7 seats), whereas in the southeast the Conservatives secured 41.4% of the vote (73 seats) to Labour's 32% (36 seats).

Such voting patterns have largely persisted into the twenty-first century, e.g. Labour won 40 of the 59 Scottish seats in the 2005 general election, with 38.9% of the popular vote across Scotland, whereas the Conservatives only secured 15.8% of the Scottish vote, winning one seat.

Participation through the ballot box

Introducing voting behaviour

Psephologists attempt to explain voting behaviour by constructing theoretical models. Different commentators favour different models, but most of the models share some common elements.

Simple voting models

The easiest way to explain voting behaviour is to think about long-term (**primacy**) and short-term (**recency**) factors. Primacy factors may predispose an individual to support a particular political party and recency factors moderate their outlook.

The primacy model

This suggests that long-term factors (e.g. class) are more important than short-term factors in deciding elections. Supporters of this view tend to see stability in electoral behaviour as opposed to volatility.

The recency model

This holds that voting patterns are in fact more volatile and that processes such as embourgeoisement have led to class and partisan de-alignment. As a result, they argue, short-term factors (issues, events, leaders etc.) are much more important, with as many as 10 million voters making up their minds in the last month of the general election campaign.

More complex voting models

Social structures model

This is effectively another way of framing the primacy model (see above). It emphasises the influence of **social cleavages** (e.g. social class, ethnicity, occupation and gender) on electoral outcomes. A belief in the enduring influence of such long-term factors would suggest that voting behaviour should be relatively stable, with fairly low levels of electoral swing between elections. This is because such social factors only change slowly.

Party identification model

Under this model individuals would identify with a political party and stick with it. For example, in the 1950s, over 90% of voters voted for either the Labour Party or the Conservatives. In the 2005 general election the figure was down to 67.5%. Those who strongly identified with either party fell from 45% in 1964 to 13% in 2001. This process of weakening party ties is commonly referred to as **party de-alignment**.

Rational choice model

This model sees voters as making considered, rational judgements on the basis of policies and issues and/or the relative attributes of the various party leaders. This may be either a **retrospective** judgement (i.e. based on past performance) or one based on a perception of how a given party might do if elected (**prospective** voting).

Issue voting is commonly sub-divided into '**spatial**' and '**valence**' models. The spatial model suggests that the parties most likely to attract voters are those who adopt the median point on the political spectrum, and thereby avoid alienating too many potential supporters. The main problem with this model is that it assumes that parties can appeal to voters simply by not offending them. In an age where parties are less ideologically based than they were in 1983, for example, there will be little to choose between them; they will both be targeting 'middle England'. The valence model therefore suggests that a party's chances of electoral success will depend upon its ability to convince voters that it can deliver on the key issues, e.g. national security, economic prosperity and law and order.

The issues that have particular **salience** (relevance) at the time of the election will have the biggest impact on voting behaviour. Parties therefore try to make sure that the issues on which they are seen as strong are the salient issues in any campaign, i.e. they seek to set the **political agenda**.

This strategy was reflected in Labour's six election pledges in 2005:

- Your family better off.
- Your child achieving more.
- Your children with the best start.
- Your family treated better and faster.
- Your community safer.
- Your country's borders protected.

These pledges aside, Labour's 2005 campaign was rather retrospective and negative, for instance reminding voters of Conservative leader Michael Howard's time in office under Margaret Thatcher ('cut services', the Poll Tax, Clause 28). In the last week of the campaign Labour warned that voting for the Liberal Democrats might let the Conservatives back in. The 2005 Conservative campaign, orchestrated by Australian consultant Lynton Crosby, was slicker than the party's 2001 effort. Crosby succeeded in shifting the focus of the whole campaign onto core issues such as immigration and law and order. The party avoided the mistake of focusing entirely on Europe, unlike William Hague in 2001 ('Seven days to save the pound'). The Liberal Democrats focused largely on such issues as public services, local taxation and Iraq.

The importance of party leaders

In 2005, 62% of election news coverage was dedicated to the discussion of issues. Much of the remaining coverage was given over to the various party leaders. The importance of party leaders in attracting voters has been on the increase in recent years. In the USA commentators often speak of a **coat-tails effect**, where the election of a popular president will also see congressional candidates from the same party returned to office. Although the UK system is somewhat different, in that we do not elect our chief executive separately, the relative popularity of party leaders (i.e. the prospective prime ministers) can have serious consequences for the party's electoral prospects. There was clearly a positive 'Blair effect' in the 1997 general election, just as Margaret Thatcher's style of leadership attracted significant numbers of voters to the Conservative Party in general elections between 1979 and 1987. Conversely, the inability of voters to picture Labour leader Michael Foot as prime minister (in 1983) and their unhappiness with Blair (in 2005) clearly put off many potential Labour voters.

The media now places far more emphasis on the words of party leaders than on other leading figures within their party. As prospective prime ministers, party leaders have to demonstrate that they have what it takes to fill the role of 'communicator in chief'.

Top politicians quoted in television and radio news in the 2005 general election campaign (number of times)

Labour		Conservatives		Liberal Democrats	
(1) Tony Blair	317	(1) Michael Howard	385	(1) Charles Kennedy	274
(2) Gordon Brown	69	(2) Liam Fox	29	(2) Menzies Campbell	40

Source: Kavanagh and Butler, *The British General Election of 2005* (Palgrave, 2005).

Dominant ideology model

According to this model, a dominant ideology benefits a ruling elite, and this elite uses its influence in the media and business to orchestrate elections to its advantage.

Voting context model

In this model, voters consider the nature of the election being contested, the importance of the resulting institution, and the workings of the electoral system in operation, before making their choice. This phenomenon can certainly be seen when comparing the results of the 2004 European elections with the general elections of 2001 and 2005. In the 2004 elections to the European Parliament, the Conservatives were the most popular choice with voters (with 26.7% of the vote), yet they were second to Labour in the general elections of 2001 and 2005. Similarly, UKIP were able to secure 16.1% of the vote in the 2004 European elections, winning 12 seats, yet in general elections they only managed 1.5% in 2001 and 2.2% in 2005.

Conclusions on voting models

Though numerous models have been advanced to explain the dynamics of voting behaviour, it is important to remember that they are not necessarily mutually exclusive, e.g. social structures might predispose an individual to support a particular party, but the 'context' unique to a particular election or the salient issues might serve to moderate their behaviour, making them more likely to vote against their natural party.

What do we mean by tactical voting and protest voting?

Tactical voting is where an individual chooses to vote for a candidate that is not his or her preferred candidate, in order to prevent the candidate they favour least being elected.

Protest voting is where voters back a candidate/party other than their normal choice in order to send a message to their 'natural' party or to the government of the day. This often occurs in elections where the outcome is less crucial to the voter, e.g. in local elections or elections to the European Parliament.

What is swing?

Swing is a measurement of the movement of votes from one party to another, between one general election and the next. It is expressed as a percentage. The national electoral swing between two parties is calculated by averaging the percentage point fall for one party and the percentage point rise achieved by the other, e.g. in 2005 the

Labour vote fell by 5.5% nationally, compared to 2001, and the Conservative vote rose by 0.6%, giving a swing of 3.05% from Labour to the Conservatives (5.5 + 0.6 = 6.1%, divided by 2 = 3.05%).

A **uniform swing** across the country would mean that a 1% swing would see all of the seats with a similarly small majority changing hands. In reality we often see **differential swing** — different rates of swing in different parts of the country. In 2005, for example, the swing from Labour to the Conservatives in Enfield Southgate was 8.7%, compared to the national swing of 3.05%.

What is churn?

Even where the swing is small (e.g. 1.8% in 2001 or 3.05% in 2005) and voting appears to be fairly stable, the headline statistics (votes and/or seats won) may serve to obscure underlying volatility. This is due to churn: where large numbers of voters switch their support between parties, between elections, while the headline statistics remain the same.

The impact of the media

The media and UK elections

The media can be divided broadly into: broadcast media (television, radio); the press (newspapers, journals, magazines); and new media (internet).

The BBC and ITC are legally required to remain politically impartial. Newspapers are free to take sides. The *Sun* was famously vocal in support of the Conservatives in the 1992 general election, coming up with such memorable headlines as 'Will the last person to leave Britain please turn out the light' when a Labour victory appeared likely. Paul Whiteley estimated that the *Sun's* decision to back Labour in 1997 cost the Conservatives around 500,000 votes.

Who did the press support in the 2005 general election?

	Daily newspapers	Sunday newspapers
Favouring a Labour victory	*Mirror, Sun, Guardian, The Times, Financial Times*	*People, News of the World, Observer, Sunday Mirror*
Favouring a Conservative victory	*Daily Express, Daily Telegraph*	*Sunday Express, Sunday Times, Sunday Telegraph*
Favouring other outcomes *Daily Mail* and *Sunday Mail* (not a Labour victory) *Independent* and *Independent on Sunday* (more Liberal Democrat MPs) *Daily Star* (no preference stated)		

The significance of opinion polls

Opinion polls are most visible at elections times. During these periods, the major polling companies (e.g. MORI and NOP) question the voting intentions of sample groups, selected with the aim of recreating a true cross-section of the electorate in a group of around 1,000 individuals. Exit polls are normally more accurate than the ordinary polls during the election campaign, because they use larger samples and ask people how they have voted, rather than surveying voting intentions. In 2005, the BBC's exit poll came within two seats of predicting Labour's actual parliamentary majority.

Do polls reflect or help to shape opinion?

In some countries (France for example) opinion polls are banned in the days leading up to elections for fear that they might influence voting intentions. Some people believe that voters are more likely to vote for parties that are doing well in the polls (the so-called **bandwagon effect**). Others argue that there is in fact a **boomerang effect**, where people vote for parties that are doing badly in the polls because they see them as the underdogs or, more likely, they do not turn out to vote when the polls show their party well ahead. Opinion poll findings can also result in an increase in tactical voting. Michael Portillo believed that his loss in Enfield in 1997 resulted, in part, from tactical voting based upon poll findings.

Poll accuracy

Even with good sampling, pollsters normally allow a margin of error of plus or minus 3%. In 1992, however, the average final poll error was 8.9%. What factors can lead to polling error?

(1) **Respondents were not registered:** in 1992 it appeared that some of those being asked the questions (the respondents) had not registered to vote, possibly in an effort to avoid the Poll Tax.

(2) **Respondents were lying:** it has been suggested that people were too embarrassed to admit publicly that they were going to vote Conservative.

(3) **Respondents were unrepresentative of the broader electorate:** sampling errors and samples that were too small meant that some surveys were skewed from the start.

(4) **Many respondents were 'floating' voters:** there was clearly a late swing to the Conservatives. Was this perhaps due to a large number of floating voters?

Media theory

Manipulative theory

This theory holds that the mass media is controlled by an elite that uses it with the sole purpose of preserving its own position, and therefore submerges a radical agenda in meaningless trivia.

Hegemonic theory

According to this theory, those who work in the media have a particular view due to their education, age, social class etc. They therefore write from a particular perspective, however unconscious their bias might be.

Pluralist theory

This theory states that what individuals choose to read and watch from the wide range of media available is based upon their own outlook and interests. The media, therefore, reflect opinion rather than shape it, thereby reinforcing views that the reader already has.

The influence of the media

Writers such as the US psychologist Leon Festinger (in the 1950s) and David Denver (in the 1980s) argued that media influence was limited by three processes: selective exposure, selective perception and selective retention.

(1) **Selective exposure:** individuals generally choose to be exposed to newspapers and television programmes that reflect, rather than challenge, their outlook.

(2) **Selective perception:** individuals mentally edit the media that they are exposed to, filtering out content that doesn't fit in with their own ideas.

(3) **Selective retention:** people tend to forget programme and newspaper content that challenges the views that they hold, while retaining material that can be used to justify their position.

Festinger maintained that individuals view media output through **filters**, with different filters being applied to different types of material. Some argue that television is so powerful because people believe what they see — their filters are effectively down when watching television. When reading newspapers, however, they are expecting bias and their filters are up.

Voting behaviour at by-elections

Large swings, low turnouts and high levels of tactical and protest voting have always been, and remain, typical of by-elections. The fact that a by-election can only in very rare circumstances precipitate a change in the government creates a situation in which voters have far greater freedom to stay at home or to cast a protest vote 'risk-free'. The media's focus on such contests also means that tactical voting is often far more prevalent.

In the last 20 years, therefore, the party of government has often been defeated when defending its own seats in by-elections. The Conservatives suffered a net loss of 22 seats in by-elections between 1979 and 1997, and didn't win a single such contest between 1989 and 1997. Though Labour did better in terms of holding its seats in by-elections after it was returned to government in 1997, low turnout and high levels of protest or tactical voting combined to produce massive by-election swings. For example in the six by-elections between 2001 and 2005 the smallest swing against Labour was 7.6% (in Ipswich) and the largest was 29.0% (Brent East). The turnout in these two contests was 40.2% and 36.2% respectively.

Electoral systems

The role of elections in a democracy

What purposes do elections serve?

Elections serve three broad and overlapping purposes within a liberal democracy.

(1) **Political recruitment:** they give citizens an opportunity to elect those individuals who will act as their representatives until the next election.

(2) **Accountability:** they provide a means by which citizens can hold individual representatives and the government of the day accountable for their actions and conduct in office.

(3) **Legitimisation:** they play a role in legitimising the government by providing the winners with an electoral mandate — be it a personal mandate for an individual MP or a broader mandate for the party that wins enough seats to secure control of the parliament or assembly in question.

What is an electoral system?

In the UK context, an electoral system is a set of rules by which popular votes are translated into seats in a legislature or a means by which an individual is chosen to fill a singular office (e.g. Mayor of London).

Electoral systems can be divided into three broad types:

(1) **Majoritarian systems:** those that require the winner to secure a majority, e.g. either the simple majority (**simple plurality**) required under first-past-the-post (FPTP) or the **absolute** (overall) majority required under systems such as alternative vote (AV) and supplementary vote (SV).

(2) **Proportional systems:** those that attempt to distribute seats in broad proportion to votes cast, e.g. list systems and single transferable vote (STV).

(3) **Hybrid systems:** those systems that combine a majoritarian and a proportional element, e.g. an **additional member system** (AMS) such as FPTP top-up or AV+.

UK electoral systems

At one time virtually all UK-based elections, whether for the Westminster Parliament, local government or UK elections to the European Parliament, were conducted under the first-past-the-post electoral system. Since 1997, however, the situation has changed markedly.

- Scottish Parliament and Welsh Assembly elections take place under a hybrid additional member system known as first-past-the-post top-up. The Greater London Assembly's 25 members are also elected under an AMS system.
- In Northern Ireland, elections to local government, the Northern Ireland Assembly and the European Parliament take place under single transferable vote, as have Scottish local elections since 2007.

- Since 1999, UK elections to the European Parliament have taken place under a closed regional party list system.
- The London Mayor and a number of other directly elected mayors around the UK (e.g. in Hartlepool) are elected under the supplementary vote system.

First-past-the-post (FPTP)

Under FPTP, voters are given a single vote which is not transferable. Votes are then counted, with the candidate securing the largest number of votes winning. A candidate need only secure one vote more than their nearest rival (i.e. a simple majority, or 'simple plurality'), even where this will often be less than 50% of the total number of votes cast for all candidates.

In the UK, FPTP normally operates on the basis of single-member constituencies, that is, where one individual is elected to represent one geographical area. In a parliamentary election this area would be called a **constituency**. In the 2005 general election there were 646 such single-member constituencies. In a local election the area represented would normally be referred to as a **ward**. In some local elections, seats may be given to more than one candidate (e.g. the two securing the most votes across the ward).

Note that where a vacancy occurs, as a result of the death or resignation of the incumbent, a by-election is held in the affected constituency/ward under the same FPTP electoral system.

FPTP and the mandate

One supposed purpose of elections is to grant those elected to government a **mandate** to govern. FPTP rarely results in a government that can claim the support of more than 50% of those who voted, yet alone 50% of the eligible voters. The last time the winning party in the general election won more than 50% of votes cast was 1935. In 2005, Labour polled only 9.5 million votes — 35.2% of votes cast (the lowest share of the vote ever recorded for a winning party at a UK general election) and only 21.6% of the electorate (another record low).

FPTP and the popular vote

FPTP only requires a candidate to secure a simple plurality of votes in order to win, rather than achieving an absolute majority. This process inevitably results in large numbers of wasted votes — those votes that make no real difference to the outcome as they are cast either for a losing candidate or for one who has already secured enough votes to win the contest. In St Albans in 2005, for example, 29,869 of the 45,462 valid votes cast were wasted.

It is also possible to win more votes nationally under FPTP (i.e. a higher share of the popular vote) and yet win fewer seats, through winning some seats by large margins and losing others by small margins. In the general elections of 1950, 1951 and February 1974, the winning party gained fewer votes nationally than the party that ended up forming the official opposition. Such results further reduce the legitimacy of the government.

Another feature of FPTP is that victory in a general election depends disproportionately on the actions of undecided or **floating voters** in a number of key marginal constituencies. Given that a candidate only needs a majority of one vote to win a seat, there is little point in parties campaigning in safe seats such as Bootle, which in 2005 had a Labour majority of 16,357 votes. It makes far more sense to focus campaign efforts on seats such as Crawley, where the winning margin was only 37 votes.

This can result in campaigns that are unduly focused on the concerns of these individuals. Note that only 62 seats changed hands between 2001 and 2005.

The debate over electoral reform

The arguments over electoral reform centre on two questions: first, whether or not the FPTP system necessitates electoral reform; and second, what model of proportional or hybrid system would best solve the defects associated with FPTP, without resulting in further, equally serious problems.

In favour of FPTP
- The system is part of our traditions.
- The system is cheap, easy to operate and easily understood. This helps voters and contributes to greater confidence in the result.
- The single-member constituency allows for a close MP–constituency link.
- The system normally produces strong, majority governments, making coalitions less likely.

Against FPTP
- The system distorts the popular vote to an unacceptable degree.
- It provides little voter choice and therefore leads to large numbers of wasted votes.
- It disadvantages small parties and those with support spread evenly across constituencies, i.e. parties who frequently come second, such as the Liberal Democrats.
- It leads to artificially polarised adversarial politics (so-called **'yah-boo' politics**). Some people maintain that coalitions would be more constructive and productive than FPTP.

The Independent Commission on Electoral Reform

In its 1997 general election manifesto, the Labour Party appeared to commit itself to a reform of the system under which general elections are contested. This decision had resulted in part from its period of 18 years in opposition, during which it appeared that the FPTP system was increasingly stacked against Labour. After the 1992 defeat, in particular, many had questioned whether Labour could ever win again under FPTP. After its victory in 1997, the New Labour administration established an Independent Commission on Electoral Reform under Lord Jenkins.

The Jenkins Report

Lord Jenkins identified a number of criteria against which electoral systems could be assessed, namely proportionality, stable government, voter choice and the MP–constituency link.

Many had expected the Liberal Democrat Lord Jenkins — one of the Gang of Four who left Labour in 1981 to found the SDP — to opt for a truly proportional system, such as a party list or STV. His eventual choice of alternative vote, with a proportional top-up (hence AV+), was the result of:

- a desire to propose a system that was moderate enough for Labour to adopt
- a recognition that a hybrid system such as AV+ would offer something on all four criteria, making it preferable to both FPTP and some of the more proportional systems in use elsewhere

Lord Jenkins's recommendation that AV+ should be introduced for UK general elections disappointed many fellow Liberal Democrats, who felt that STV might be more effective in addressing the flaws in the current FPTP system. Despite this, Labour decided not to move ahead. A number of factors might explain this decision.

Why wasn't the Jenkins Report implemented?

- The introduction of alternative systems in other UK elections had not been met with universal approval.
- New systems had cost Labour dearly in the Scottish Parliament, Welsh Assembly and European Parliament.
- Reform appeared less necessary now that Labour had been elected under FPTP with a good Westminster majority.
- FPTP appeared to be disadvantaging the Tories more than Labour. It was said that Labour would win a clear majority in the Commons, even if the Tories won an equal share of the popular vote.
- It was estimated that, if Lord Jenkins's proposed system (AV+) had been operating in 1997, the actual Labour majority of 179 would have been reduced to 60.

Other electoral systems

Single transferable vote (STV)

STV is a proportional system used in many elections in Northern Ireland, in Scottish local elections (since 2007) and in Eire. It aims to improve voter choice, achieve clear proportionality and eliminate wasted votes through a complex system of vote transference.

STV employs large multi-member constituencies. Voters may indicate as many prefer-ences on their ballots as there are seats to fill in their constituency, by numbering their choices (1, 2, 3 etc.). In order to be elected, a candidate must achieve a quota, which is normally calculated using the **Droop formula**:

$$\frac{\text{Total valid votes cast}}{\text{Seats in constituency} + 1} + 1$$

Thus in the example of a five-member constituency, a candidate would need to secure a sixth of the votes plus one, as such a quota could only be achieved by five candidates.

Once a quota is met, surplus votes for that candidate are transferred in accordance with second preferences. Where no candidate is elected on first preferences, the bottom candidate is eliminated and their votes are redistributed. This process continues until all of the available seats have been filled.

The impact of STV in the UK

It is widely accepted that the majority of voters in Northern Ireland do not fully understand the workings of STV. This lack of intelligibility could be said to undermine confidence in the system, as could the time sometimes taken to finalise results. That said, STV has clearly brought significant benefits to Northern Ireland.

First, STV has resulted in more proportional electoral outcomes than was the case under FPTP. This is particularly true of the way in which STV has operated in respect of elections to the Northern Ireland Assembly. For example in 2003, Sinn Fein secured 23% of first preference votes and 24% of seats, with the SDLP winning 17% of first preferences and 18% of seats.

Second, by rewarding parties on both sides of the religious divide more fairly, the system has given rise to coalitions in the Northern Ireland executive. Though in the short term the system appeared to polarise opinion, STV has helped to enhance representation and reduce sectarianism — as evidenced by Reverend Ian Paisley (DUP) becoming first minister with Sinn Fein's Martin McGuinnes as his deputy.

Would the use of STV in UK general elections change electoral outcomes?

It is often said that STV would benefit parties at the centre because they would gain significant support when votes are transferred. This belief assumes that Labour and Conservative voters will put Liberal Democrat candidates down on their ballot papers as their second preference (or lower). In reality, the supporters of these parties might just as easily cast all of their votes for other candidates standing for their preferred party.

It is also argued that a system such as STV will inevitably lead to coalition government. The experience in Eire, where there has normally been one-party majority government, shows that factors such as the prevailing political culture and the existing party system may be as important as the electoral system in determining electoral outcomes.

Academics from London and Essex 'reran' the 1997 general election under a range of systems using 8,000 voters. This **Essex Model** suggested that Labour would have had a majority of 25 under STV, compared to the actual majority of 179 that it secured under FPTP. That said, one should remember that 1997 was one of the biggest landslide victories on record, and coalitions would probably be the norm if STV were to be used in UK general elections.

content guidance

Hybrid systems

Hybrid systems such as the additional members system award a proportion of the seats available on a majoritarian basis (e.g. using FPTP or alternative vote) with the remainder being allocated on a proportional basis (e.g. using a party list). Hybrid systems seek to retain the strong MP–constituency link and majority government commonly associated with majoritarian systems, while introducing more voter choice and a greater degree of proportionality.

Examples of hybrid systems
- **Additional member system (AMS):** this is used in Germany. Fifty per cent of seats are elected under FPTP, with the remainder distributed proportionally. There is a threshold of 5%, which parties must cross before they are entitled to any of the additional seats.
- **First-past-the-post top-up (FPTP-TU):** a variant of AMS that is used in elections to the Scottish Parliament, the Welsh Assembly and the Greater London Authority.
- **Alternative vote plus (AV+):** the system proposed by the Jenkins Commission.

Case study: the impact of AMS in elections to the Scottish Parliament

Under the AMS used in elections to the Scottish Parliament, two-thirds (73) of the 129 seats are awarded on a constituency basis under FPTP, with the remaining one-third (56) distributed as a top-up under a regional list system employing a variation of the D'hondt formula. The top-up element of the AMS used in Scotland has proved fairer to those parties that do not have enough support to win in a single FPTP constituency, e.g. the Scottish Socialists and the Greens. It can also benefit larger parties in certain circumstances. The Conservatives, for example, secured 18% of the vote in Scotland in the 1997 general election, yet won no Scottish seats in the Westminster Parliament. In the 1999 Scottish Parliament election, they similarly failed to win a single FPTP contest, but were awarded 18 top-up seats. In the 2007 elections they performed more creditably in the constituency contests but still gained most of their seats as a result of the regional top-up (see the table below).

The 2007 elections to the Scottish Parliament

Party	Constituencies % votes	Seats won	Regional lists % votes	Seats won	Totals
Conservative	16.2	4	13.9	13	17
Labour	32.2	37	29.2	9	46
Lib Dem	16.6	11	11.3	5	16
SNP	32.9	21	31.0	26	47
Green	–	–	4.0	2	2
Others	2.1	0	10.6	1	1
	Totals	73		56	129

Would the use of AMS in UK general elections change electoral outcomes?

Though some argue that AMS can result in a two-class system of representatives — some with constituencies, some without — its introduction in UK general elections would certainly allow for more proportional electoral outcomes. That said, such hybrid systems do not allow the degree of proportionality offered by pure list systems or STV. This is because they seek to deliver on the full range of criteria identified by Lord Jenkins, rather than prioritising proportionality above all else.

Although AMS would tend to result in a more stable government than that formed in the wake of an election held under a purely proportional system, it is still likely that the introduction of AMS in UK general elections would result in coalition government. In the Essex Model, Labour would have fallen 27 seats short of a Commons majority under the AMS system used in the research. Furthermore, the experience under AMS in Scotland suggests that the existence of such coalition governments would have significant impact on the scope and extent of government policy, e.g. the Labour–Liberal Democrat coalition administrations in place in Scotland from 1999 to 2007 moved to introduce free long-term nursing care for the elderly, abolish top-up fees, and introduce a more effective Freedom of Information Act.

Party list, supplementary vote and alternative vote

The specification mentions FPTP, STV and AMS by name. You therefore need a thorough working knowledge of these systems in order to tackle the questions that are likely to turn up on the paper. That said, you will also need an outline knowledge of other majoritarian and proportional systems that are used in the UK and elsewhere.

You need to know how list systems work in order to understand the 'top-up' element of the AMS system used in the UK. A knowledge of the supplementary vote and alternative vote systems will be of use when answering more general questions on the arguments for and against electoral reform.

Party list

List systems are party-based as opposed to candidate-based. This is because voters express a preference for a party rather than a candidate, with seats then being awarded to each party in proportion to its share of the popular vote from a list of candidates drawn up by the party in question.

A **national list** system is more proportional yet all but removes the MP–constituency link, as all MPs would theoretically be representing one big national constituency. A **regional list** system would maintain a link between each representative and their region, but it can result in some parties being under- or over-represented in relation to their share of the popular vote.

Each party's list is normally **closed**, i.e. the party decides the order of candidates on its list with voters having no say. An **open list** system allows voters to choose between a given party's candidates, rather than simply voting for the party and letting the party hierarchy decide the order of candidates. This increases voter choice.

A **threshold** is a percentage of the vote that a party must secure before it wins any seats under a list system. Thresholds are used to prevent the kind of fragmented legislature that can result from lots of small parties each winning a handful of seats. Thresholds therefore sacrifice a little proportionality in favour of more stable government, although a very low threshold, such as the 1.5% bar used in elections to the Israeli Knesset, will still result in many smaller parties winning seats.

What is the impact of party list in the UK? British elections to the European Parliament take place every 5 years and have operated under a closed regional list system since 1999. The 2004 UK elections to the European Parliament demonstrate the way in which parties that would be unlikely to win seats under FPTP can prosper under a more proportional system: UKIP won 12 seats and the Greens returned two MEPs. That said, the regional list system still favours parties with clearly defined areas of support (e.g. Plaid Cymru) over those whose support is spread more evenly across the country (e.g. the BNP).

Would the use of a party list system in UK general elections change electoral outcomes? As a pure proportional system, an open national list with no threshold would result in far more parties being represented in the House of Commons and no single party having an overall majority. The result would be a coalition government, with the stability of that coalition dependent upon just how many parties had to be brought on board in order to command a Commons majority.

According to the Essex Model, Labour would have secured 285 seats if such a pure proportional system had been used in 1997. This would have seen it fall 89 seats short of an overall majority, though the party would have been able to form a majority administration with the support of the 110 Liberal Democrat MPs who would have been returned under the system.

Supplementary vote

The supplementary vote (SV) system is a majoritarian system. Though it may result in an allocation of seats that *appears* more proportional nationally for parties such as the Liberal Democrats, it is not a proportional system. There is no guarantee that small parties will be better rewarded than they are under FPTP.

SV works by voters expressing a first and second preference when voting. If no candidate receives more than 50% of first preferences, all but the top two candidates are eliminated, with their votes transferred to second preference candidates where they are still in the race.

AV is similar to SV in that it employs preferential voting. Both systems allow a candidate to win outright where they can secure over 50% of first preferences. The two systems differ in respect of what happens when no single candidate has an absolute majority of first preferences. Under SV, as we have seen, the votes of all but the top two candidates are transferred on the basis of their second preferences. Under AV, candidates would be eliminated one by one from the bottom, with votes being transferred until one of the remaining candidates was able to secure an absolute majority.

It is clear that SV serves to reduce wasted votes and increase voter choice, while retaining the strong MP–constituency link that exists under FPTP.

There are, however, a number of more specific observations that can be made. Under the supplementary vote:

- **the centre-left is favoured** by allowing Labour voters to select Liberal Democrats as a second preference and Liberal Democrat voters to do the reverse. SV has therefore served to undermine the chances of Conservative candidates who might once have gained from votes on the centre-left being split.
- **tactical voting is reduced** because voters have the benefit of a second preference.
- **winners can have less than 50% of the vote.** The winning candidate under SV is not guaranteed to have at least 50% of the popular vote, because the ballots of eliminated candidates will only be transferred if their second preferences are for one of the two remaining candidates.
- **voters have to use guesswork.** In a race between four or more candidates, voters effectively have to guess which two candidates will be left in the final run-off before casting their votes, e.g. in the first London mayoral contest in 2000, the official Labour candidate Frank Dobson was eliminated after the first preferences were counted. This is one reason why the Electoral Reform Society originally favoured the use of AV over SV in such mayoral contests.

The nature of representation

What is representative democracy?

The Anglo-Irish politician Edmund Burke summed up what many see as the essence of representative democracy in Britain in a speech to his Bristol constituents in 1774: 'Your representative owes you not his industry only but his judgement,' Burke argued, 'and he betrays you if he sacrifices it to your opinion.' The Burkeian view, therefore, is that we elect individuals to represent us in Parliament and other assemblies, and they then represent our interests to the best of their ability until the next election. They are not delegates sent with specific instructions or orders to follow. As a result, our elected representatives might make decisions that are contrary to our wishes. This representative form of democracy is often referred to as **indirect democracy**.

What is direct democracy?

Direct democracy is said to have its origins in classical Athens (*c.* 500 BC), where the city-state's 40,000 free men had the right to attend forum meetings at which certain policies could be approved or rejected. The classic modern tool of direct democracy is the **referendum**.

What is a referendum?

A referendum is a vote on a single issue, normally in the form of a question requiring a yes or no answer. Unlike the kinds of initiatives used in the USA and elsewhere (see below), referendums are normally top-down, government initiated votes, in some cases seeking approval for a policy that has already been legislated for.

Referendums in other countries

Outside the UK referendums are used to resolve a wide range of issues. In Eire, for example, a 1995 referendum legalised divorce, whereas in Switzerland, which averages around four referendums per year, the people approved a decision to join the UN by 55% to 45% in 2002.

What is an initiative?

In many countries citizens have the right to initiate their own referendums when they can raise enough signatures on a petition. Many US states allow these kinds of initiatives (often called **propositions**). Though not all of these measures pass, many do, e.g. Proposition 184 in California created a mandatory 25-year sentence for those convicted of a serious felony for the third time (the so-called 'three strikes and you're out' rule). Many other countries have similar provisions. In Italy a referendum can be initiated with the support of 500,000 of the country's registered electors, whereas in New Zealand the Citizen's Initiated Referenda Act (1993) required support of only 10% of the electorate in order to initiate a non-binding referendum.

UK referendums

In the 1940s the then prime minister, Clement Attlee, described referendums as devices 'alien to our traditions'. What did he mean?

First, the UK is said to operate, by tradition, under a system of representative democracy (see above). Under this system governments are elected to make decisions on behalf of citizens. The idea of government asking citizens to make a binding decision through a referendum would appear to undermine this idea of representative democracy.

Second, at the time that Attlee made his remarks the UK had not held a conventional referendum. Such devices were, therefore, literally not part of our traditions.

When are referendums called in the UK?

Though the lack of a codified constitution means that we have no formal list of circumstances in which referendums are legally required, it has long been accepted that such votes can, and probably should, be called in respect of major constitutional changes.

There has only been one UK-wide referendum, the ballot held on continued membership of the EEC (now the European Union) in 1975, though the whole UK has since been promised votes ahead of the proposed UK adoption of the euro and, more recently, the ratification of the EU constitution (see pp. 46–47). Whereas other nations regularly hold referendums on issues ranging from the availability of abortion to their membership of NATO, all nine referendums sanctioned by the UK Parliament since 1973 have related to the distribution of power between regional (i.e. sub-national), national, and supranational levels of government (see below).

UK referendums, 1973–2007

Date	Who voted	Question	% yes	% no	% turnout
1973 (March)	Northern Ireland	Should Northern Ireland stay in the UK?	98.9	1.1	58.1
1975 (June)	UK	Should the UK stay in the EEC?	67.2	32.8	63.2
1979 (March)	Scotland	Should there be a Scottish parliament?	51.6	48.4	63.8
1979 (March)	Wales	Should there be a Welsh parliament?	20.3	79.7	58.3
1997 (Sept)	Scotland	Should there be a Scottish parliament?	74.3	25.7	60.4
		With tax-varying powers?	63.5	36.5	
1997 (Sept)	Wales	Should there be a Welsh assembly?	50.3	49.7	50.1
1998 (May)	London	Should there be a London mayor and London assembly?	72.0	28.0	34.0
1998 (May)	Northern Ireland	Approval for the Good Friday Agreement	71.1	28.9	81.0
2004 (Nov)	Northeast England	Should there be a regional assembly for the northeast?	22.0	78.0	48.0

Case study: calls for a referendum over ratification of the 2004 EU constitution

The debate as to whether or not there should be a UK referendum to approve the treaty establishing the new EU constitution illustrates the way in which such devices can become more about party politics than about enhancing political participation.

Labour's changing position on the need for a referendum on the EU constitution

(1) Initially Labour saw no need for a referendum, arguing that the constitution was merely a 'tidying up exercise', necessitated by the widening and deepening of the European Union.

(2) Public pressure and promises of referendums made by the Conservatives and Liberal Democrats just before a likely election forced the prime

minister's hand. Consequently, Labour went into the 2005 general election promising a referendum on the EU Constitution.

(3) The rejection of the treaty by voters in referendums in France and Holland in 2005 allowed Jack Straw to announce that plans to hold a UK referendum had been postponed.

(4) The constitution was replaced by a 'Reform Treaty' which, the government argued, did not warrant a referendum.

Case study: calls for a referendum over the 2007 EU Reform Treaty

Calls for UK ratification of the Reform Treaty (later dubbed the Lisbon Treaty) to be subject to a nationwide referendum resulted largely from the obvious similarities between the new document and the constitution that it replaced.

David Cameron's Conservatives supported calls for a referendum, ostensibly on the basis of their contention that the Reform Treaty was the constitution in all but name. However, their support for a public vote also had the benefit of creating greater unity within their own ranks, while at the same time putting Gordon Brown on the back foot during a period when the new prime minister and his party were enjoying a healthy lead in the polls.

Tony Blair had claimed that Tory calls for a public vote over the Reform Treaty were 'utterly absurd' — a position maintained by Gordon Brown after he became prime minister in June 2007. Both leaders believed that the new treaty simply tidied up some of the loose ends that had resulted both from earlier treaties and from the enlargement of the European Union from 15 to 27 states between 2004 and 2007.

Labour's position was made difficult, however, first by the August 2007 opinion polls that showed 80% of the general public favoured a vote, and second by the position taken by the TUC. The unions' primary concern was the UK opt-out from the proposed charter of rights, which would see citizens in the other 26 EU member states being granted enhanced rights in respect of industrial action. Many delegates at the TUC September conference were also keen to see the government honouring its 2005 commitment to hold a referendum over the original constitution.

Future UK referendums?

A referendum is still likely before entry into the single European currency (euro). Since 1997, the Labour Party has been committed to a referendum before any change is made to the electoral system used in UK general elections. It is likely that referendums would also be employed to decide other key constitutional changes concerning institutions such as the monarchy.

Arguments for and against the wider use of referendums in the UK
For referendums
- Referendums offer a more direct form of democracy. They encourage participation by allowing citizens to have a real input on key decisions that matter to them, e.g. on the adoption of the euro.

- They provide a way of focusing or renewing the mandate on a particular issue or legitimising major constitutional changes, e.g. the referendums held ahead of the creation of the Scottish Parliament and Welsh Assembly.
- They can prevent dangerous divisions within political parties over controversial issues. This prevents governments from collapsing and, therefore, provides greater continuity in government, e.g. the way in which the 1975 referendum on UK membership of the EEC minimised the damage done by divisions within the Labour Cabinet.
- They could be used to provide a clear and final answer where parliament is deadlocked.
- They could provide a method for resolving tricky moral questions.

Against referendums

- Referendums are inconsistent with our system of parliamentary government. They undermine representative democracy by allowing governments to duck their responsibility to govern. This can result in a tyranny of the majority.
- Far from encouraging participation, regular use of referendums could lead to apathy and low turnouts that might distort the results, e.g. the turnout in the 1997 referendum over the creation of a Welsh assembly was only 50.1%. In extreme cases this can result in the tyranny of an organised minority.
- They undermine collective responsibility in cabinet, e.g. during referendum campaigns such as that in 1975, collective responsibility is suspended over the issue in question in order to allow full public debate of the issues involved.
- Most issues are too complicated to be condensed into a simple yes/no question. For example, should the decision over joining the euro be in the hands of the general public or those with some grasp of economics?
- Funding differentials between the 'yes' and 'no' camps might mean that the referendum is not played out on a level playing field, e.g. it was said that the 'yes' campaign in 1975 was far better funded than the 'no' camp.
- Governments can schedule referendums and phrase questions in a way that makes a favourable result more likely. Some argue that the question posed in 1975, 'Should the UK stay in the European Community?', encouraged a yes vote because people were more likely to vote in favour of the status quo (i.e. against change). A more neutral question would have been 'Should the UK be part of the European Community?'
- Decisions are not always considered final. Governments sometimes go back again and again until they get the result that they want, e.g. the creation of a Scottish parliament was put to the vote twice (in 1979 and 1997).

Changes to the way in which referendums operate

Though critics of referendums argue that results are too often skewed by the precise phrasing of the questions posed, the timing of the poll, and the funding of the 'yes' and 'no' campaigns, many of these issues have been addressed — at least in theory — by the creation of the **Electoral Commission**. The precise wording of any future referendum would have to be approved by the Electoral Commission, in order to avoid any dangers associated with biased wording. Lord Neill's **Committee on Standards in Public Life** (1998) also argued that future referendums in the UK should be state funded and that the 'yes' and 'no' campaigns should share a £1.2 million pot.

Political parties
The role of political parties in a democracy

Definitions

A political party is an organisation whose members share a common ideology and/or policies, and come together to seek election to political office. Most parties would ultimately aim to win general elections and form governments. It is in this last respect that parties differ from pressure groups. Pressure groups do not normally themselves seek election, though some groups employ electoral candidacy as a means of raising public awareness, even though they have little realistic chance of being elected. In recent years such groups have included the Referendum Party and the Pro-life Alliance.

The Green Party: political party or attitude cause group?

It is possible for one or more pressure groups to evolve into a political party. A good case in point is the Green Party. Known before 1985 as the Ecology Party, the Green Party's origins can be found in a pressure group called 'People' that was formed in 1973. Though the Green Party itself initially appeared to be little more than a glorified single-issue group, it has developed a broader range of policies in recent years in order to improve its electoral prospects.

The origins of the UK party system

Before the 1832 Great Reform Act, parties did not exist as mass-membership organisations with formal structures outside parliament, but as groups of like-minded individuals within the legislature, bound together by ideas, friendship or family ties. With electoral reform, however, came a need to organise and mobilise the expanding electorate.

Party roles

It is said that political parties serve five main roles:
(1) **Representation:** traditionally parties represent the views of their members.
(2) **Participation:** parties allow individuals to participate at all levels.
(3) **Political recruitment:** parties play a role giving future leaders their political apprenticeship. Candidate selection processes cast aside the unsuitable.

(4) Policy formulation: parties debate and formulate policy, before presenting it in a coherent programme (the manifesto).

(5) Providing stable government: without parties, it is argued, the Commons would simply be a gathering of over 600 individuals.

Party systems

The two-party system

Most commentators characterise Britain as operating a two-party system, where two fairly equally matched parties compete for power and smaller parties have no realistic prospect of breaking the monopoly held by the two big ones. The rise of the Liberals and their allies since 1974 in terms of percentage share of the vote, linked to periods of dominance by either the Conservatives or Labour, suggests the end of the two-party system.

Is Britain a two-party system?

The arguments in support are:

- The Labour and Conservative Parties are the only parties that have a realistic chance of forming a government in the near future or being the senior partner in a coalition.
- Even in 2005, the Labour and Conservative Parties secured 67.4% of the popular vote and 86% of the 645 seats contested.
- The Liberal Democrats (in third place) are still a long way behind the second party.
- There has been a good deal of stability in elections. Only 10% of seats changed hands in 2005.

The arguments against are:

- The UK is a dominant party system (see below).
- In 2005, 32.6% of voters backed other parties.
- Though the Liberal Democrats are a third party, they are often second to Labour in the north and west and to the Conservatives in the south and east.
- The apparent stability in voting ignores significant churn.
- Any party that could mobilise non-voters (38.6%) could win the election.

Other types of party systems

The single-party system

This is where a single party dominates, banning other parties and exercising total control over all candidates if elections should occur at all, e.g. Nazi Germany.

The dominant-party system

Where many parties exist but only one holds government power, e.g. Japan under the Liberal Democratic Party (1955–93). Between 1979 and 2005, the UK experienced a long period of Conservative dominance (election victories in 1979, 1983, 1987 and 1992) followed by a period of New Labour dominance (election victories in 1997, 2001 and 2005). Some people now argue, therefore, that the UK has become a dominant-party system.

The multi-party system

In a multi-party system many parties compete for power and the government will often pass between coalitions formed by different combinations of parties (e.g. Italy from 1945 to 1993).

The Conservative Party

The origins of the party

The Conservative Party emerged from the Tory Party in the 1830s. Many date its birth to Robert Peel's Tamworth Manifesto (1834). In the twentieth century, the party was in office (either alone or in coalition) for 67 years and enjoyed two extended periods in office:

- 1951–64 under Churchill, Eden, Macmillan and Home
- 1979–97 under Thatcher and Major

Party ideology

One-nation Tories

For most of the twentieth century the party was truly conservative in ideology, i.e. rooted in pragmatism and the belief in gradual improvements founded on experience and existing institutions rather than *a priori* reasoning and radical change. This was a form of collectivist or paternalist conservatism that favoured pluralism and social inclusion, and maintained that, though authority should be centralised, the state should be benevolent and care for the most needy.

The proponents of this form of conservatism, now commonly referred to as one-nation Tories, were committed to: a mixed economy (Keynesianism); more significant state intervention, where necessary; slow gradual change — evolution not revolution; internationalism and increasing European integration; and support for a universal welfare state.

Thatcherism

The late 1970s and early 1980s saw the rise of a new form of liberal or libertarian conservatism on both sides of the Atlantic. Dubbed the 'New Right', this movement combined a belief in free market economics and deregulation (dubbed **neo-liberalism**), with support for traditional social conservatism, i.e. support for the traditional family unit, religion and traditional views on sexual orientation. US President Ronald Reagan (1981–89) and UK Prime Minister Margaret Thatcher (1979–90) were key figures in this movement, to the point that it has commonly become known simply as Thatcherism in the UK. Supporters of this form of conservatism favoured the importance of the individual over the needs of society, and supported: free market economics; deregulation; privatisation of nationalised industries; restrictions on the power of the unions; limited state intervention ('rolling back the frontiers of the state'); quick and radical change; maintaining national sovereignty; and more limited welfare provision (a low 'safety net').

Thatcher dubbed those who were not prepared to sign up to this agenda, most often the old one-nation Tories, the **'wets'**. Committed Thatcherites were commonly referred to as **'dries'** — with her most loyal henchmen being dubbed 'ultra-dry'.

Conservative factions and groups

The factional infighting that came to the fore as a result of this shift in direction under Margaret Thatcher led to formal challenges to her leadership of the party in 1989 (by Anthony Meyer) and 1990 (by Michael Heseltine). Though Heseltine's challenge led to Thatcher's resignation (in November 1990), a succession of Conservative leaders since then — Major, Hague, Duncan Smith, Howard, Cameron — have failed to command the full confidence of the whole parliamentary party. This is due to internal party factions and personal rivalries. Though Philip Norton identified seven broad and overlapping factions within the parliamentary Conservative Party in the 1990s, most commentators still prefer to identify more straightforward cleavages:

- One-nation Tories, 'wets', Europhiles, e.g. Tory Reform Group (1975)
- Thatcherites, 'dries', Eurosceptics, e.g. Bruges Group (1988)

Cameron and the 'New Tories'

David Cameron's election as party leader in 2006, following three successive general election defeats (in 1997, 2001 and 2005), was widely seen as the kind of watershed or epiphany that the Labour Party had experienced a decade earlier under Tony Blair. Cameron's election was significant because it marked the point at which rank and file members recognised the need to choose a leader who could appeal to those outside the party — and thereby win an election.

Cameron sought to lead the Conservatives away from areas of policy over which the party was deeply divided (e.g. Europe) and towards those where it could gain electoral advantage. This shift to the centre saw the party attempting to lead the way on issues such as climate change. The desire to challenge the perception that the Conservatives were the 'nasty party' was also reflected in former Conservative leader Iain Duncan Smith's foundation of the Centre for Social Justice in 2004. This organisation's early reports, Breakdown Britain and Breakthrough Britain, offered the prospect of the party becoming more receptive to strategies aimed at addressing poverty and social exclusion.

Such developments saw many commentators drawing parallels between the leader/shadow chancellor team of Cameron/Osborne and that of Blair/Brown in the early days of New Labour. As a result, many dubbed Cameron's party the 'New Tories' or, as Cameron himself put it on at least one occasion, 'liberal conservatives'.

The Labour Party

The origins of the party

The Labour Party was created at the start of the twentieth century. Though the Independent Labour Party, the Fabians and the Social Democratic Federation were also involved in forming the Labour Representation Committee in 1900, it is important not to underestimate the role of the Trade Union Congress (TUC). In 1900, 94% of the Labour Representation Committee's affiliated membership was from the unions, and they still controlled around 80% of the votes at party conference and provided a similar proportion of the party's income in the early 1990s.

The Labour Party was formed to represent the working classes at a time when the franchise had not yet been extended to such groups. The decision to give all men over 21 the right to vote in 1918 provided the Labour Party with the potential base of support necessary to launch a serious electoral challenge.

Party ideology

The party's origins in the unions and socialist societies of the late nineteenth and early twentieth centuries meant that it originally pursued an orthodox socialist agenda.

The Labour Party constitution of 1918

The extension of the franchise to all adult men coincided with the adoption of the new Labour Party constitution (1918). Clause IV of this constitution provided clear commitments to public ownership of key industries and the redistribution of wealth:

> ...to secure for the workers by hand or by brain the full fruits of their industry and the most equitable distribution thereof that may be possible upon the basis of the common ownership of the means of production...

Despite its left-wing origins, by the 1970s the party was home to a number of ideological factions. For example, the prime minister James Callaghan and those on the right of the party took the view that public sector pay demands had to be resisted, whereas those on the left (e.g. Michael Foot and Tony Benn) favoured greater wealth redistribution.

Labour's defeat in the 1979 general election, following the Winter of Discontent, saw those on the left gain control of the party, under the leadership of Michael Foot. Foot led Labour into the 1983 general election with one of the most left-wing manifestos in the party's history. It included a commitment to state control of all major industries, tighter regulation of business, enhanced workers' rights, support for unilateral nuclear disarmament and withdrawal from NATO. Widely dubbed 'the longest suicide note in history', the manifesto was seen as a key factor in the Conservative Party's landslide victory, though others (e.g. the Falklands factor) were also crucial.

New Labour

Though the Labour Party was formed to represent the working classes, changes in class and occupational structures since the 1960s and the general election defeats of 1979, 1983 and 1987 saw the party looking to broaden its appeal beyond this core support.

This process of outreach, started by leaders such as Neil Kinnock (leader 1983–92) and John Smith (1992–94), is most closely associated with the leadership of Tony Blair (1994–2007). Under Blair, the party was rebranded 'New Labour', with the old Clause IV being removed from the party's constitution in 1995. Some accused Blair and other Labour modernisers of abandoning the socialist principles upon which the party was founded.

The Liberal Democrats

The origins of the party

The Liberal Democrats were formed in 1988 with the merger of the Liberal Party and the Social Democratic Party (SDP). The Liberal Party had been the main party of government in the early twentieth century but was a distant third party by the 1960s, rarely polling more than 10% of the vote. The SDP, in contrast, had been formed as a result of the decision of leading Labour politicians to leave the party in 1981. Roy Jenkins, David Owen, Bill Rogers and Shirley Williams felt that the Labour Party had come under the control of hardline left-wingers following the defeat of James Callaghan's moderate Labour administration in 1979.

This **Gang of Four**, as they were known, launched the SDP with their Limehouse Declaration in 1981. With the Labour Party in disarray, the SDP formed an electoral alliance with the Liberals (the SDP–Liberal Alliance) in 1983, securing 26% of the popular vote yet only gaining 23 seats in Parliament. Following a similarly disappointing return for the Alliance in 1987, the parties merged in 1988 to form the Social and Liberal Democrats, with Paddy Ashdown elected as leader. The following year the party renamed itself the Liberal Democrats.

Party ideology

Whereas conservatives traditionally emphasise the role of society in shaping individuals, liberals place a greater emphasis on the importance of the individual. Liberal society is to be formed of free individuals, autonomous and equally valuable.

'Classical liberalism'

Nineteenth-century liberalism, now commonly referred to as 'classical liberalism', saw minimal state intervention as being the ideal. There was an emphasis on freedom, tolerance and equality: individuals were seen as rational beings who had choices to make, and liberals favoured self-help and self-improvement. In the latter half of the twentieth century, many aspects of classical liberalism were adopted by the New Right. Those at the vanguard of this movement (e.g. Margaret Thatcher) were therefore often referred to as being neo-liberal.

'New' or 'progressive liberalism'

Over time, this classical view of deregulated 'small government', where people interact freely, was tempered by a realisation that, without regulation, abuses could occur. The market could not be allowed to go unchecked — self-help would not be enough. There was a need for state provision of schools and hospitals. Pensions and unemployment benefit could and should be provided. Such ideas were put forward by writers such as T. H. Green and later L. T. Hobhouse. John Maynard Keynes and William Beveridge provided the basis for the mixed economy and welfare state of the postwar years (i.e. from 1945).

This more progressive form of liberalism — with its emphasis on reform, individual rights, and a mixed economy — has provided the ideological foundation for all of the liberal centre parties of the second half of the twentieth century, most recently the Liberal Democrats.

Liberal Democrat MPs in Parliament

The Liberal Democrats have increased their representation in the Commons since 1992, although they are still hugely under-represented in relation to their share of the popular vote. The party has been particularly successful in by-elections, during periods of both Conservative and Labour government, perhaps due to the numbers of protest and tactical votes they attract as a centre party.

Liberal Democrat performance in general elections

Year	% of popular vote	% of seats won	Number of MPs
1992	17.8	3.1	20
1997	16.8	7.0	46
2001	18.3	7.9	52
2005	22.0	9.4	61

The Liberal Democrats in government?

Though the party has not been part of the government at Westminster — alone or in coalition — it has been involved in coalition executives in Scotland and, for a time, in Wales. In Scotland, in particular, the Liberal Democrats were able to force concessions on a number of policies while in coalition with Labour (1999–2007), e.g. on top-up fees and free nursing care for the elderly.

The 'end of ideology' and the rise of 'catch-all parties'?

As we have seen, UK parties were once said to be ideologically based. In recent years, however, they are said to have abandoned their traditional ideologies as part of an effort to appeal to as wide a range of voters as possible. Though it is probably fair to say that UK parties were always broad churches, these modern catch-all parties are criticised as being little more than election-winning machines.

Party organisation

The Labour and Conservative Parties at a local and national level

Those who join the Labour Party are assigned to a local branch according to their postal address. These local branches are the lowest level of the party organisation. They have a role in selecting candidates for local elections as well as sending delegates to the General Committee of the Constituency Labour Party (CLP).

The CLP plays a key role in organising the party at constituency level. It takes the lead in local and national election campaigns and still plays a part in selecting parliamentary candidates, though the extension of one member one vote (OMOV) has diminished this role.

The National Executive Committee (NEC) is the main organ of the national party. It ensures the smooth running of the party, oversees the preparation of policy proposals, has the final say on the selection of parliamentary candidates, and enforces party discipline. The party's annual conference was once the sovereign policy-making body within the Labour Party, though its role was diminished somewhat in the 1990s (see below).

The Conservative Party has a similar structure locally. Branches corresponding to local council wards operate at the lowest level. Above the local branches are the constituency associations. These bodies play a key role in organising the party at the grassroots level, planning election campaigns, and selecting parliamentary candidates. As is the case with the Labour Party, however, the constituency associations do not have the same free rein in selecting parliamentary candidates that they once had (see below).

How parties operate at a European level

UK members of the European Parliament (MEPs), who numbered 78 in 2008, sit in a number of transnational (as opposed to a single national) groups within the chamber. Conservative MEPs sat with the Group of the European People's Party and European Democrats (EPP-ED) following the 2004 European Parliament elections, as did the single Ulster Unionist MEP; Labour MEPs sat with the Socialist Group (PES); and the Liberal Democrats sat with the Alliance of Liberals and Democrats.

Internal party democracy: policy formation

Conservative Party
The party leader retains the major role in policy-making within the party, though he/she is expected to take on board the views of others, e.g. the front bench, the 1922 Committee, party elders and the grassroots membership. The Fresh Future initiative launched by William Hague aimed to make policy-making more inclusive. Two new bodies, the National Conservative Convention and the Conservative Political Forum, were created, though both remain largely advisory in nature.

Labour Party
The party conferences of the past were genuine policy-making events. From 1997, however, the party adopted a 2-year policy-making cycle. The National Policy Forum appointed policy commissions to make proposals, which were then to be formalised in the National Executive Committee (NEC) before passing to the party conference for approval. This afforded the party leader more control and helped the party avoid nasty surprises at conference.

Liberal Democrats
The party is federal in structure, comprising English, Scottish and Welsh state parties that head a further four, three, and three tiers respectively. Decisions are taken at the most appropriate level. The biannual federal conference is the supreme policy-making body in the party. It deals with policy proposals from the federal policy committee, state, regional and local parties. The party leadership has a good deal of control over the federal policy committee.

Internal democracy in policy-making vs 'electability'
Though many political parties are keen to appear to be involving their ordinary

members in the formation of party policy, they are painfully conscious of the fact that they need to have policies that appeal beyond their paid-up members if they are to have any chance of being elected. In an age of mass-membership parties, the views of members might have been a fair indication of how the broader public would react to a given policy. In the modern era, however, party membership is falling and those who do join are increasingly unrepresentative of the broader population. In this context, allowing members to determine policy could amount to electoral suicide.

Are the Liberal Democrats too internally democratic in terms of policy-making?
Though the Liberal Democrats have the most democratic method for determining party policy, some argue that the resulting policies (e.g. on cannabis possession, asylum seekers and the local income tax) were rather too easily picked off by Labour and Conservative activists in the 2005 campaign. Several anti-Liberal Democrat websites have turned the party's own policies against them.

Internal party democracy: selecting parliamentary candidates

Parties and political recruitment
A role commonly attributed to political parties is that of political recruitment. It is argued that parties play a role in training potential candidates (through their involvement in grassroots party activity). Potential candidates thus serve a kind of political apprenticeship within the party.

Separating the wheat from the chaff
The number of individuals wanting to be elected to parliament far exceeds the number of Commons seats available. Even within a given political party one would expect to see a handful of willing candidates for every seat contested, hence the need for short-listing (see below). Parties play a key role in separating the genuine contenders from the no-hopers.

Selection procedures
All three major parties employ a similar three-stage process in selecting parliamentary candidates:
(1) Hopefuls must appear on a centrally vetted and approved list of prospective candidates.
(2) The local party draws up a shortlist from those approved candidates who have expressed an interest.
(3) Those attending a meeting of constituency members (as in the case of the Conservatives) or all constituency members by ballot (for Labour and the Liberal Democrats) vote for their preferred candidate.

The deselection and imposition of candidates
Though constituency parties in all three major parties are normally allowed the final say in selecting their parliamentary candidates from the nationally approved lists, the national parties retain the ultimate power to deselect and impose candidates where they see fit.

Under Neil Kinnock, Labour deselected a number of sitting MPs in 1986 for being part of the banned Militant Tendency. They included Dave Nellist and Terry Fields. The party has also imposed its preferred candidates on constituencies from time to time, e.g. former Conservative MP Shaun Woodward in St Helens.

The Conservative MP Sir Nicholas Scott (Kensington and Chelsea) was deselected by his constituency party in December 1996 following a series of alcohol-related incidents. In the run-up to the 2005 general election, Michael Howard first sacked and then expelled party deputy chair Howard Flight from the Conservative Party for publicly undermining the party's manifesto commitments on taxation.

Internal party democracy: choosing party leaders

One significant indicator of internal party democracy is the extent to which regular members are given an input into the process by which the party leader is chosen.

The Conservative Party

From 2001 the selection of Conservative leaders was a two-stage process. First, MPs were balloted, with the bottom candidate being eliminated at each ballot until only two candidates remained. Then regular party members were given the chance to make a choice between the final two candidates on an OMOV basis.

Does the system work?

The problem with this system, which was part of William Hague's efforts to democratise the party's internal processes, is that Conservative MPs can manipulate the final choice presented to rank-and-file members by voting tactically in the initial ballots. In 2001, for example, those on the right of the party deliberately switched their votes in the final ballot of MPs in such a way as to eliminate the early favourite, Michael Portillo, and present the rank-and-file members with a choice between the Eurosceptic Iain Duncan Smith and the moderate Kenneth Clarke — a candidate whom Duncan Smith's supporters knew would not be able to defeat their man in a ballot of individual party members.

Duncan Smith's failure to command the full support of the parliamentary party in the year following his election as leader cast doubt over the whole process for electing Conservative leaders. As a result, the rank and file were effectively excluded from the process of electing his successor in 2003, with Michael Howard's so-called 'coronation'.

The Labour Party

The process by which Labour leaders are chosen involves an electoral college made up of three equal parts: one-third of the votes are held by the parliamentary party (including MEPs); one-third are held by affiliated organisations (mostly unions); and the final one-third are cast by members of constituency Labour parties on an OMOV basis.

The Liberal Democrats

The Liberal Democrat system for choosing leaders is generally regarded as being the most democratic, as it operates under an STV system using OMOV. Those wishing to stand must also be proposed and seconded by fellow MPs and nominated by no fewer than 200 members from at least 20 different local parties.

Party funding

Traditional sources of party finance

All main parties receive income in the form of membership subscriptions. Until the 1990s, however, the lion's share of Labour Party funding came from fees paid by trade unions and other affiliated organisations. The Conservative Party was said to be bankrolled by wealthy business interests.

The changing basis of party funding

The decline of UK political parties as mass-member organisations has had an adverse impact on party finances. By the 1990s, the RSPB had more members than all three main UK parties. The efforts to reduce the influence of trade unions within the Labour Party under Kinnock, Smith and Blair also resulted in falling revenues. Such developments led parties to court donations from wealthy individuals (e.g. Bernie Ecclestone and Lord Sainsbury for Labour, and Sir Paul Getty and Stewart Wheeler for the Conservatives).

The best parties money can buy?

The rise of large individual donations to political parties since the 1990s led to the perception that one might be able to 'buy influence', in much the same way that Mohamed Al Fayed claimed to have done with individual Conservative MPs such as Neil Hamilton in the closing years of John Major's time in office. Some felt that Bernie Ecclestone's £1 million donation to the Labour Party in 1997 may have resulted in the subsequent delay in the introduction of the ban on tobacco advertising in Formula 1.

The Political Parties, Elections and Referendum (PPER) Act

The PPER Act (2000) placed overall limits on party spending in general election campaigns (£30,000 per constituency) as well as requiring that nationally, parties have to publicly declare all donations over £5,000. In so doing, the act sought to make parties less reliant on wealthy individual backers, and to challenge the perception that politics was 'for sale'. Despite these changes, Labour, the Conservatives and the Liberal Democrats still declared £9 million, £8 million and £4 million respectively in donations in 2005.

The loans for peerages scandal

The Labour Party sought to entirely circumvent the PPER's regulation of donations by encouraging supporters to offer the party long-term, low-interest loans instead of donations. It was this tactic, and the inducements supposedly offered to secure such lines of credit, that gave rise to the 'loans for peerages' scandal.

The Philips Report

Two reports were published in the wake of these events. The first, Party Funding (2006), was produced by the Constitutional Affairs Select Committee. The second,

Strengthening Democracy: Fair and Sustainable Funding of Political Parties (2007) — the 'Philips Report' in shorthand — came at the end of a government-initiated review conducted under the chairmanship of Sir Hayden Philips. Significantly, both reports concluded that one way forward might be greater state funding for UK political parties, with the Philips Report offering the prospect of some form of 'pence-per-voter' or 'pence-per-member' funding formula.

Should political parties be state funded?

It is commonly argued that state funding of political parties would serve to reassure voters. There are a number of arguments for and against this view.

Arguments for:
- If parties are not funded by taxpayers, they will be funded by interest groups.
- State funding would allow politicians to focus on representing their constituents.
- It would also mean that parties such as the Liberal Democrats could finally compete on an equal financial footing.

Arguments against:
- Why should taxpayers bankroll parties that they may not support?
- Politicians could become isolated. It is good that interest groups are at the heart of government.
- Parties will always have unequal resources, even if finances are tinkered with in this way.

Though the case in favour of the comprehensive funding of UK political parties was still not universally accepted by January 2008, it is worth remembering that partial funding was already in place by that time (see the box below).

State subsidies to political parties: some recent examples

- In 2006–07, the three main parties each received almost £456,000 from the state's Policy Development Fund (set up by the Political Parties, Elections and Referendum Act 2000).
- At Westminster, opposition parties in 2006–07 received over £6 million of 'short money' (designed to help meet the cost of their administration and other parliamentary business).
- During 2006–07, the parties' television election broadcasts received subsidies worth £16 million (having been £68 million during the general election year of 2005).
- At the 2005 general election, the parties' postal costs were met by a grant of £20 million.

Source: P. Fairclough, R. Kelly and E. Magee, UK Government & Politics Annual Survey 2008 (Philip Allan Updates, 2008).

The rise of minor parties in elections

Recent years have witnessed a marked increase in the support given to minor parties and single-issue candidates at elections.

Single-issue parties

The Green Party

In the 1999 European elections the party secured 6.3% of the votes and returned two MEPs under a regional party list system, a result it repeated in 2004. In the 2005 general election the party secured 1% of the popular vote in England and Wales nationally. In Brighton Pavilion its candidate Keith Taylor came third (21.9% or 9,530 votes).

British National Party (BNP)

The party has done well in the northwest in recent local and parliamentary elections. In 2005, however, its support increased in other areas. The party secured 0.7% of the vote nationally in 2005, winning its largest share of the vote in Barking, where its candidate Richard Barnbrook was third with 4,916 votes (16.9%), just 27 votes behind the Conservatives. The party also won shares of 10%+ in Dewsbury and Burnley.

UK Independence Party (UKIP)

In 2004 the party increased its share of the vote to 16% in the European elections (from 7% in 1999), winning 12 seats (three in 1999). It also gave a creditable performance in the 2001 and 2005 general elections. In 2005 it put up candidates in 495 parliamentary constituencies, securing 2.2% of the vote nationally. The party's leader, Roger Knapman, secured 7.7% of the vote in Totnes. UKIP's campaign was inevitably undermined by Robert Kilroy-Silk's decision to leave and form his own party, Veritas.

Single-issue candidates

The last three general elections have witnessed the rise of single-issue candidates alongside single-issue parties, e.g. the election of Martin Bell as an anti-corruption candidate in Tatton in 1997 and Dr Richard Taylor as the Kidderminster Hospital and Health Concern candidate in Wyre Forest in 2001 (re-elected in 2005). One factor that might explain this phenomenon is the extent to which mainstream parties have ceased to fulfil their representative function.

Single-issue and independent candidates returned to parliament in 2005

Name	George Galloway	Peter Law	Richard Taylor
Cause	Respect	Independent	Independent Kidderminster Hospital and Health Concern
Constituency	Bethnal Green and Bow	Blaenau Gwent	Wyre Forest
Majority	2,879	9,313	9,293

Nationalist parties in Scotland and Wales

Scottish National Party (SNP)

The party was formed in 1934 and has the central aim of achieving an independent Scotland. It campaigned for a 'yes, yes' vote in the 1997 referendum, supporting the creation of a devolved parliament with tax-varying powers.

Though the SNP performed creditably in the Scottish Parliament elections in 1999 and 2003, it was excluded from government by the Labour–Liberal Democrat coalition that was in place from 1999. In the 2007 Scottish Parliament elections, however, the SNP campaigned for a referendum on the question of full independence for Scotland, securing 47 of the 129 seats available (one more than Labour). The party's failure to secure a coalition partner in the wake of the elections meant that it was forced to go into government alone, forming a minority administration with its leader, Alex Salmond, taking on the role of first minister.

Plaid Cymru (PC)

The party was formed in 1925 with the central aim of achieving an independent Wales. It also aims to encourage the preservation of Welsh culture and, in particular, the use of the Welsh language.

Though the party's efforts to achieve a degree of self-government for Wales were dealt a blow by the failure of the 1979 referendum on Welsh devolution (only 20% 'yes' on a 58% turnout), the party campaigned strongly for a 'yes' vote in the 1997 referendum that established the Welsh Assembly (50.3% 'yes' on a 50.1% turnout). The party performed reasonably well in the assembly elections in 1999 and 2003.

Regional parties at Westminster

Though devolved parliaments or assemblies have been established in Northern Ireland, Scotland and Wales, nationalist parties are still elected to represent their constituencies in the Westminster Parliament. Some regard this as a problem, particularly with regard to Scotland (the so-called West Lothian question), where primary legislative powers over many aspects of policy are now held by the Scottish Parliament but MPs representing Scottish constituencies in the Westminster Parliament still sit and vote on policies that will not directly affect their constituents. The decision to reduce the numbers of Scottish seats in the 2005 general election (by 13) was a stop-gap rather than a final solution.

Regional party performance in the 2005 general election

- Plaid Cymru's share of the vote fell relative to 2001. It won three seats, and was down one.
- The SNP share of the vote also fell, but it won six seats, a notional gain of two.
- The Democratic Unionists won nine of the 18 seats in Northern Ireland, gaining four seats. They polled more votes in Northern Ireland than any other party. Sinn Fein won five seats, up one on 2001. The SDLP won three seats, unchanged in net terms, while the Ulster Unionists were left with one seat, down five on their 2001 performance.

Source: House of Commons Research Paper 05/33

Pressure groups and protest movements

Pressure groups, political communication and policy-making

Definitions

Pressure groups are groups of like-minded individuals who campaign for their collective interests and/or in pursuit of a common cause.

Pressure groups are significantly more numerous than political parties because they have a tendency to fragment opinion, whereas political parties tend to aggregate and accommodate a wider range of views in an effort to be elected. In recent years there has been a rise in the popularity of smaller, more focused, single-issue groups, over the larger, more traditional sectional and cause groups. Such groups often only seek to represent the interests of a very small group of individuals or to focus on a cause that is limited in breadth and time (e.g. efforts to prevent specific construction projects such as a road or a runway). Some see this rise of single-issue politics as a fundamental change in the nature of political participation within the UK.

Pressure group roles

(1) Encouraging and enabling participation. Pressure groups provide people with an avenue for non-electoral participation between elections.
(2) Representing their members' sectional interests or advancing a common cause, by aggregating and articulating the common interests/concerns of a given group of individuals.
(3) Acting as a source of specialist knowledge. They help governments weigh up the merits and demerits of proposed policies, thereby avoiding costly mistakes and unnecessary confrontation.

Types of pressure group

Classification by aims (the sectional/cause group typology)

Sectional groups

These groups seek to protect the interests of a particular section of society. They are therefore sometimes referred to as '**interest**' or '**protectionist**' groups.

Such groups' membership is normally exclusive, as their membership is usually restricted to the section of society whose interests they serve. A teachers' union such as the NASUWT, for example, will represent the interests of its members who will, for the most part, be practising teachers.

Cause groups

These groups seek to promote a particular cause. As a result they are sometimes referred to as '**promotional**' groups. Unlike most sectional groups, they seek a broader membership and do not necessarily stand to benefit directly from their campaigns. This makes them more inclusive.

There are three sub-categories of cause groups:

Attitude cause groups	Aim to change peoples' attitudes on a particular issue. Greenpeace, for example, seeks to change attitudes on the environment.
Political cause groups	Aim to achieve certain political goals, e.g. Charter 88.
Sectional cause groups	Protect a section of society, e.g. Shelter works on behalf of the homeless but its members are not all homeless.

Problems with classifying groups by aims

Classifying groups by aims tends to ignore the fact that many groups campaign for a cause as well as representing the interests of their members. Teaching unions, for example, would claim to be working for broader improvements in education policy as well as representing the sectional interests of their members. The subdivision of cause groups is similarly problematic. The division between some attitude and political cause groups is far from clear cut, and the line between sectional groups and sectional cause groups is similarly blurred.

Classification by status (the insider/outsider group typology)

Problems with classifying pressure groups by aims (i.e. as sectional/cause groups) have led writers such as Wyn Grant to suggest that it is more helpful to classify groups according to their status in relation to the government.

Insider groups

These groups have better access to government.

- Those that have strong two-way relationships with policy-makers over a broad range of issues (e.g. the BMA, the NFU) are called '**core insiders**'.
- Those who are granted such status within a more narrow area of expertise (e.g. the WWF) are known as '**specialist insiders**'.
- The third group, '**peripheral insiders**', are those who have insider status but are only rarely needed by government due to the nature of their interest/cause (e.g. the Canine Defence League).

Outsider groups

Outsider groups are similarly divided into:

- **potential insiders** — those who are outside due to the nature of their cause, or their inexperience, e.g. Charter 88, before 1997
- **outsiders by necessity** — those who are unlikely to achieve high status and must work outside, e.g. CND or Fathers4Justice
- **ideological outsiders** — these include groups such as Amnesty International, who prefer to remain outside the system

Problems with classifying groups by status

Classifying groups by status (i.e. insider/outsider) addresses some of the problems inherent in classifying by aims and may also be more helpful in assessing the likelihood of a group achieving its central aims.

Such labels, however, ignore the fact that many groups can operate to some extent as both as insiders and outsiders, and that groups can move quickly from outside to inside and vice versa.

Charter 88 was clearly outside the political loop before the 1997 general election but has assumed more influence following Labour's victory. In contrast, as Wyn Grant has noted, the NFU's insider status came under threat over the course of the same period.

Factors affecting group success

A pressure group's success is commonly measured in terms of the extent to which a group achieves its objectives. If we accept this definition, a group's chances of success will depend upon a number of factors:

(a) Group aims

Achievability
- *High*, e.g. renovating a children's play area
- *Low*, e.g. securing a global ban on nuclear power

Public receptivity
- *High*, e.g. saving an endangered species
- *Low*, e.g. improving conditions in prisons

(b) Group status, e.g. insider/outsider

(c) Group methods

(d) Group specialism and expertise, e.g. RoSPA, RSPB, Electoral Reform Society

(e) Group resources
- human — e.g. size of membership (large membership can help provide finance and bigger groups can organise more effective mass-campaigns), skills of members (PR skills, practical skills, legal expertise)
- financial — e.g. membership groups often rely on membership fees; groups representing powerful interests may have a lot of money; fundraising events, donations etc. are also important

Problems with measuring a group's influence

The effectiveness of pressure group activity is hard to gauge. This is because highly successful and privileged insider groups are unlikely to publicise the extent of their influence, for fear of alienating the government and losing their status. In the same light, high-profile protests and stunts might appear impressive, but succeed only rarely in changing policy. Even during the fuel protests in 2000, the government chose to speak to the Road Hauliers' Association, rather than to those organising the protest.

Pressure groups and the EU

Many pressure groups turn to the European Union when:
(1) they are faced with a national government that is unsympathetic to their cause
(2) their sectional interest or cause is supranational

Environmental pressure groups and the EU

Environmental pressure groups have two good reasons to focus their attention on Europe rather than solely on their national governments.

First, environmental issues by definition do not respect national boundaries. It therefore makes more sense to deal with environmental issues at a European or international level than simply at a national level.

Second, the EU is already committed to environmental protection and is, therefore, more sympathetic to the aims and objectives of many environmental pressure groups than are national governments.

In the broad areas of economic and environmental policy the proliferation of Europe-wide regulation provides an opportunity for real influence not often afforded pressure groups at a national level. On issues such as the improvement of water quality, for example, UK environmental groups have made great progress by working through the EU. Many beaches in England, previously categorised as unfit for bathing due to sewage pollution, have been improved under pressure from Europe. Groups such as Surfers Against Sewage (SAS) have played a part in bringing about such changes. The policy of awarding blue flags for clean beaches has also had the effect of raising the public profile of the EU. But despite all of this, business interests remain better funded and better equipped to put their case than most environmentalists.

As the EU becomes more involved in aspects of common social and foreign and security policy, a wider range of UK pressure groups are likely to turn to Europe.

The growing power of the EU

Under the European Communities Act (1972), European law takes precedence over national laws where the two are in conflict. Pressure groups can therefore force change on their national governments by going over their heads.

Since 1986, decisions made by the Council of Ministers have increasingly been taken under a system of **qualified majority voting** (QMV) rather than unanimity. This means that groups must work to build up a broader European support, rather than simply lobbying their own governments to block measures using the national veto. Though QMV makes life more complicated for pressure groups, it does bring with it some real advantages. A UK-based group can, for example, campaign for a measure affecting the UK in the knowledge that the UK government alone cannot prevent it from happening.

The importance of Eurogroups

If pressure groups in each member state conducted their activities independently, their voices might be lost. As a result, like-minded pressure groups often aggregate their efforts, forming 'Eurogroups' that possess sufficient resources and represent a large enough 'constituency' for their views to be heard. The scale of the EU means that there are many points of leverage where pressure can be applied. The European Commission, for example, has a massive appetite for information and recognises Eurogroups as a legitimate source of information. The most successful Eurogroups will need the resources to make the most of these opportunities. A permanent EU office is the ideal, though not all groups can afford a permanent office in Brussels.

The National Farmers Union (NFU) has a permanent office in Brussels, but it is also a member of **COPA-COGECA**. COPA is the umbrella organisation representing the main agricultural organisations in the EU. COGECA is the equivalent organisation for agricultural cooperatives. In 2005, COPA-COGECA had 69 member organisations, representing around 11 million farmers across the EU.

Pressure group behaviour

Pressure group methods

The nature of pressure group activity will depend greatly upon the scope and extent of each group's objectives. Pressure groups can make use of a range of access points. Those groups whose aims are local and limited in scale may be able to achieve their goals without ever needing to engage with central government. Broader-based environmental groups will, in contrast, need to work at local, national and supra-national levels in order to achieve their objectives.

What are access points?

Access points (or 'points of leverage') are the points within the political system at which pressure groups and other interested parties can exert pressure on those who hold political power. In a unitary system, where power is concentrated at the centre, access points tend to be less numerous than in a federal system, where sovereign power over different areas of policy is held at different levels of government. Systems that incorporate a clear separation of powers and an entrenched system of checks and balances (e.g. the USA) are likely to offer pressure groups a greater range of meaningful access points than those systems where powers are fused and the checks on the executive are weak (e.g. the UK). In recent years, however, a number of factors have served to increase the range of access points available to UK pressure groups, e.g. the establishment of a Scottish parliament with primary legislative powers in a range of areas; the creation of assemblies and executives in Wales, Northern Ireland, and London; and the creation of a more independent UK Supreme Court, separate from the House of Lords.

Traditional methods

Many pressure groups still use traditional methods such as letter-writing campaigns, petitions and marches, and conventional lobbying. The anti-abortion organisation Life, for example, compiled a petition of more than 2 million names in the mid-1980s and employed postcard campaigns in 1989 and 1990 against the Human Fertilisation and Embryology Act. Marches against the Poll Tax in 1990 were also influential.

What is lobbying?

In its broadest sense, lobbying is, as John Kingdom put it, the 'act of seeking the ear of a member of government'. At a simple level individuals or members of pressure groups may write to a government minister or visit the Palace of Westminster to lobby in person those who have influence over the group's area of interest or expertise. In the modern era it is more common for groups to work through professional lobby firms. For a fee these organisations will direct professional lobbyists to use their contacts on behalf of the pressure group in question, e.g. the one-time lobbying group Ian Greer Associates arranged the initial contact between Mohamed Al Fayed and the then Conservative MP and junior trade minister Neil Hamilton.

Influencing the legislative process directly

Some groups have regular contact with government over a broad range of related issues. These core insider groups have the ability to influence the formation of policy at an early stage through consultation with ministers, civil servants and government-appointed bodies working on legislative proposals. Many larger groups employ lobbyists to pursue their legislative goals and some maintain permanent Westminster offices.

Embarking on legal action

Legal action can be an effective, if expensive, pressure group tactic. Such action can work in two ways:

- First, where the court finds that the government has acted in a manner beyond the authority granted it (**ultra vires**).
- Second, where such action raises public awareness of a particular issue, win or lose, e.g. the Pro-life Alliance's challenges over the application of the Human Fertilisation and Embryology Act (1990).

Working through a political party

Pressure groups can cultivate links with political parties with a view to influencing the formation of policy. When a party is in government this is usually harder to achieve, because the government is likely to be subject to far greater demands on its time and policy-formation is often more 'top-down'. The easiest time for pressure groups to gain a foothold within parties is when they are in opposition, e.g. the relationship between Charter 88 and Labour pre-1997.

Direct action campaigns

Direct action is an increasingly popular form of pressure group action. It starts from the premise that conventional methods of influencing policy are flawed and that more visible and direct protests, even involving illegal methods or violence, may offer the best opportunity of success because they make politicians take notice and can broaden public support.

Though many feel that direct action techniques provide the most immediate way of articulating their views and achieving tangible results, critics argue that the rise in single-issue, direct-action politics undermines our system of representative democracy. This is because such campaigns prevent governments from implementing their programmes and from pursuing policies that address the bigger picture.

The scope and scale of direct action campaigns has increased significantly since the 1990s. The anti-roads protests of recent years (see below), the campaign against live animal exports, the campaigns against fox-hunting and vivisection, the fuel protest and campaigns by groups such as Fathers4Justice have all been seen to have some effect on policy or opinion.

Managing the media

Groups increasingly employ sophisticated media techniques to advance their cause or sectional interests. They can use paid media, taking out whole-page advertisements in the national press, using direct-mail or producing and airing television advertisements, e.g. during the 1997 general election the Referendum Party produced a video, which it sent free of charge to millions of households. Established caring charities have also made use of such tactics. Barnardo's ran a series of hard-hitting magazine advertisements depicting the fate of vulnerable children. The NSPCC also used television advertising in their Full Stop campaign targeting violence against children. Groups can also use unpaid media, eliciting news coverage by organising stunts, planning marches, or employing direct action techniques.

Case study: the media war over the Brent Spar

In 1995 Shell gained permission from the government to dump the 14,500 ton Brent Spar oil platform in the North Atlantic. Greenpeace opposed the decision and at the time was also looking for a symbol that could be used to focus attention on the planned European environmental summit. Greenpeace activists boarded the Spar and specialised climbers made it secure. They flew in a satellite uplink, turning the Spar into a floating television station that could broadcast live to European news programmes. Greenpeace also: flew in reporters to film Shell's attempts to remove activists from the platform; organised parallel boycotts and protests at Shell petrol stations in Germany and Holland; and issued press releases providing compelling, if not always accurate, data on the residues inside the Spar. This approach effectively won the propaganda war, with Shell shelving its plans to dump the platform. Greenpeace had thereby achieved its twin goals of raising the profile of the summit and preventing the Spar being dumped.

Pressure group case studies

Environmental groups

Environmental pressure groups range from massive international groups (e.g. Greenpeace), many of which are part of Eurogroups that lobby at a supranational level, down to small groups campaigning against the removal of trees from local parks.

Some are clearly insider groups, though not always powerful core insiders. The World Wide Fund for Nature, the RSPB and the RSPCA, for example, will all find themselves consulted by the government. For example, the RSPCA was consulted over the Dangerous Dogs Act (1991). Others groups such as road protesters or the Animal Liberation Front are firmly outside the political loop, the road protestors because its aims run contrary to government policy and the liberation front because its extreme tactics cause its members to be classified more as animal rights terrorists than as belonging to a legitimate pressure group.

Direct action has been a key environmental pressure-group tactic in recent years, e.g. Swampy (Daniel Hooper) dug himself into tunnels as part of direct action anti-road protests. Such protests resulted in multi-million pound delays that, it is argued, forced the government to rethink its road-building strategy.

Trade unions

The 1970s was a decade of high union membership and militancy: the National Union of Mineworkers (NUM) were widely credited with paralysing Edward Heath's Conservative government, and the so-called Winter of Discontent (1978–79) led directly to the fall of James Callaghan's Labour Government.

Why did this change?

- **Changing occupational structure:** the decline in heavy and manufacturing industry led to the decline of what Ivor Crewe called the traditional or old working class in favour of a new working class that was less cohesive, less militant, and less heavily unionised.
- **Anti-union legislation in the 1980s:** various employment acts and trade union acts pushed through during the Thatcher years (1979–90) severely limited the unions' ability to act quickly and freely, e.g. forcing unions to hold secret ballots before strike action and banning secondary or sympathy action. The defeat of the NUM in 1985 following a year-long strike marked a watershed in union power.
- **Labour Party reform:** Labour's introduction of OMOV (1993) saw the party take a significant step away from the power of the union block-vote. The reform of the Labour leadership election process has also reduced union power, as did the party's ability to attract major business backers.

Unions in the twenty-first century

Many felt that the return of the Labour Party to government in 1997 would herald a change in the fortunes of trade unions following 18 years of Conservative government. In reality, however, the nature of the economy, the labour market, and Labour's unwillingness to reverse the anti-union legislation of the 1980s, made progress for the unions relatively slow. Only around one in five private sector workers were union members in 2005.

Internal pressure group democracy

Pressure groups are said to play a vital role in a liberal democracy as they provide avenues for representation and participation. But despite this, many groups are not internally democratic.

Internal democracy and legitimacy

The level of internal democracy present in a group may have a bearing on its legitimacy. As Wyn Grant notes, 'We need [to be able] to ask questions about whom they represent and how their policies are arrived at'. Though some groups are clearly engaged in intense internal debate (e.g. the RSPCA over fox-hunting), others such as Greenpeace are entirely centralised, despite having large individual memberships.

How are pressure group officers chosen?

In many cases pressure group officers are appointed rather than elected by the group's members on an OMOV basis. This means that those leading pressure groups are often not directly accountable to members.

How do pressure groups make decisions?

In many pressure groups key decisions are taken not by members, but by a central committee or board which is itself unelected. Neil McNaughton suggests that groups such as the BMA and the AA are particularly poor at consulting their members over questions of policy and direction, and that the organisation of many groups, therefore, reflects elitism rather than pluralism.

Some sectional groups, for example trade unions, have been forced to become more internally democratic as a result of employment and union legislation passed in the 1980s (e.g. the requirement to hold ballots before national strike action). Other sectional groups (e.g. non-membership groups) may have little internal democracy. Many cause groups start as a small group of committed individuals and control often remains with these individuals, or their chosen successors, even when the group's membership expands significantly.

Greenpeace

According to Wyn Grant (2002), Greenpeace is a hierarchical organisation that allows little democratic control over the direction of its campaigns.

- It has a strictly bureaucratic, if not authoritarian, internal structure.
- A small group of people has control over the organisation, both at the international level and within national chapters.
- Local action groups, which exist in some countries, are totally dependent on the central body.
- The rank and file is excluded from all decisions.

Are pressure groups good for democracy?

Yes

(1) Pressure groups occur naturally under any system of government. People have a natural desire to unite in protection of their own interests or in advancing a particular cause.

(2) Pressure groups allow people to organise and articulate their views between elections.

(3) Groups provide an additional avenue for participation, at a time when some other more traditional forms (e.g. party membership and voting) are waning.

(4) Pressure groups allow a wider range of opinions to be represented than is possible through political parties, particularly in a post-ideological age of catch-all parties.

(5) Groups play an essential role in moderating the views of their more extreme members. Without such groups, individuals with extreme views might never have their views challenged and changed.

(6) They allow the strength (i.e. intensity) of opinions to be expressed, as opposed to simply counting the number of people supporting a view — as happens at elections.

(7) They play a role in educating the public and providing the government with expertise.

No

(1) The quality of participation offered by pressure groups is often low, even where group membership is high. Many members do little more than pay their annual membership fee. This is referred to as 'passive membership'.

(2) Many pressure groups lack legitimacy because they exhibit low levels of internal democracy.

(3) Many non-membership groups are simply fronts for wealthy and influential business interests who may have little interest in the greater public good. This is true of many core insider groups.

(4) Pressure groups do not compete on an equal financial footing. Poorer groups find it far harder to access the policy-making process.

(5) Human resources are also an issue. Groups tend to be more successful when they have articulate, educated leading members. Many have argued that this tends to favour groups run by the middle classes over those set up by the working class, for the working class. We should really be talking about elites theory rather than pluralist theory.

(6) Groups often have an effect on government that is disproportionate to their size or to the merit of their cause. By using direct action, and even illegal tactics, groups can defeat the efforts of popularly elected governments and change policy. The views of a small minority of the population should not be given a disproportionate influence on the decision-making process, undermining long-term planning and joined-up government.

(7) Are groups 'educating' or 'misleading' the government and the broader public? Though most cause groups really do believe in what they are saying, this does not mean that the information they provide is wholly free of bias. Groups can use their access to government to distort the evidence base upon which policy is founded.

Questions
&
Answers

This section of the book looks at a range of answers to the kinds of questions you may face in your Unit 1 examination. It is divided into the four content areas identified in the specification: participation and voting behaviour; electoral systems; political parties; and pressure groups and protest movements.

For each of these four areas, there is a typical three-part (45-minute) AS question. Each question is accompanied by two model answers: one of A-grade standard and the other of C-grade standard. None of the answers given here is intended to be perfect. Each simply represents one way of approaching the question given, with an indication of the grade that it might achieve.

Immediately after each question, before the student answer, you will find a brief 'examiner's advice' section, which outlines the focus and scope of the question. Following each answer there is an 'examiner's comment' (indicated by the symbol ℮), dealing with the main plus points and minus points of the answer. You will also find shorter examiner's comments interspersed throughout the answers. Read all of the examiner's advice and comments sections carefully. They will give you an idea of what you need to do in order to get an A-grade equivalent mark for the question or sub-question. The commentaries will also help you to become more familiar with the three assessment objectives given in the Introduction to this guide.

As is the case with any study aid, this book is aimed at helping you to develop your work — rather than helping you to avoid it! It is far better for you to attempt the questions provided here without first reading the student answers given. Once you have done this, you can then review your work in light of the examiner's advice and comments provided. Remember that these student answers are *not* model answers for you to learn and reproduce word for word in the examination. It is unlikely that the questions in the examination will be worded exactly as they are here and, in any case, there is always more than one way of answering any question.

Participation and voting behaviour

Read the extract below and answer parts (a) to (c) which follow.

> **The media and elections**
>
> The media can be divided into three broad categories: print media (i.e. the press); broadcast media (i.e. television and radio); and new media (e.g. the internet). Of these three forms, it is the activities of the press, specifically newspapers, which get the most attention at election time. Some argue that the **opinion polls** published in the press during campaigns serve to shape, as opposed to simply reflecting, public opinion. Moreover, newspapers are not legally required to remain impartial and most, if not all, take up clear party positions during election campaigns. The *Sun* was particularly vocal in support of the Conservatives in the 1992 general election, coming up with such memorable headlines as 'Will the last person to leave Britain please turn out the light' when a Labour victory appeared likely. Both Neil Kinnock (the then Labour leader) and Norman Tebbit (a former leading Conservative) believed that the tabloid press were crucial in bringing about the surprise Conservative victory in that year.
>
> Source: adapted from P. Fairclough, *AS & A-Level Government and Politics*, Oxford University Press (2006)

(a) Explain the term 'opinion polls' used in the extract. (5 marks)

(b) Using your own knowledge as well as the extract, examine two or more ways in which the media can affect electoral campaigns. (10 marks)

(c) 'Long-term influences on voting behaviour such as social class no longer play a significant role in determining the outcome of **UK** elections.' Assess the accuracy of this view. (25 marks)

(a) A clear definition is the key to a good part (a) answer. Once you have this in place, you can demonstrate your understanding by bringing in material both from the extract and from your own knowledge, e.g. the stimulus material raises the possibility that opinion polls may shape as well as reflect the public mood. You could pick up on this, using your own knowledge to make passing reference to 'bandwagon' and 'boomerang' effects.

(b) It is important to develop a range (i.e. two or more) areas when answering this question. Do not fall into the trap of simply developing the material on opinion polls that you introduced in part (a). Where possible, support each point that you make with examples from recent elections.

(c) This question is not simply about the link between social class and voting. It is asking you to put class into its proper context alongside other long-term influences on electoral behaviour (e.g. age, gender, education), before offering an assessment of whether or not such long-term factors remain decisive. This final judgement can only be made if you also consider some short-term influences on voting (e.g. salient issues).

■ ■ ■

A-grade answer

(a) Opinion polls are surveys of public opinion on specific issues. They are most visible at election times, when major polling companies such as MORI question the voting intentions of sample groups of eligible voters. The extract says that opinion polls may shape as well as reflect opinion. This is because some voters are more likely to vote for parties that are doing well in the polls, creating a 'bandwagon effect', whereas others may stay at home on election day if they think that their party is well ahead (creating a 'boomerang effect'). This is why the French ban such polls in the run-up to elections. Opinion polls may also encourage tactical voting.

> 🖉 The candidate provides a clear and concise definition of the term as well as making explicit reference to the extract ('shape as well as reflect opinion'). With all five marks here awarded for AO1 (knowledge and understanding), the candidate's ability to make use of their own knowledge (MORI, bandwagons/boomerangs, France) can be fully credited. This response would score **full marks**.

(b) One obvious way in which the media can affect the outcome of electoral campaigns is by commissioning and publishing opinion polls. As the extract points out, such polls not only reflect but also shape public opinion. Voters may want to be 'part' of a winning team. The 'feel good' factor that results from a party clearly making good progress in the polls can draw in more support. Voters are also far more likely to support candidates and parties who they think have a realistic chance of winning. Opinion polls can help voters to form judgements about a candidate's electability. Opinion polls may also make tactical voting more likely. Michael Portillo believed that his loss in Enfield in 1997 was partly the result of tactical voting based upon early poll findings.

The second way in which the media can have an effect on campaigns is simply by reporting what happens in the campaign, what the parties are saying or doing. Even when it is presented in a more neutral way, on the television news for example, such coverage can do a great deal to affect electoral outcomes. For example, coverage of Neil Kinnock's address at the Labour Party's Sheffield rally was said to have damaged the party's chances in 1992 — just as the reporting of then Tory deputy-chair Howard Flight's remarks over Tory tax plans ahead of the 2005 general election undermined Michael Howard's attempt to maintain party unity.

The third way in which the media can affect the campaign is by coverage that is openly biased for or against a particular party. The press (i.e. newspapers) have far more latitude in this area. The extract mentions the *Sun*'s famous headline in 1992 ('Will the last person to leave Britain please turn out the light'). It is widely accepted that such coverage damaged Labour's chances in that year's general election. The fact that five daily papers supported Labour in 2005, with only two backing the Conservatives, might have been a factor in that election.

There is an argument, however, that people just select the media that fits in with the views that they already hold. Would someone who was really pro-immigration choose to read the *Daily Mail*? Do many core Conservative supporters read the *Guardian*?

> ✍ The candidate provides a clear focus on the question from the outset, dividing the discussion into a number of distinct areas. The opening paragraph overlaps a little with part (a), but this is not a problem as long as the material is relevant to both sub-questions — as it is here. Relatively few candidates would be able to recall this many relevant examples under test conditions, and such knowledge would score highly on AO1. The allusion to media theory (selective exposure) in the closing paragraph could be developed further, though this is still a **top-end A-grade** response without such detail.

> Note that this is probably a little long for a part (b) response. Writing too much in response to questions carrying relatively few marks can cause problems later on in the exam.

(c) In the 1960s Pulzer famously concluded that 'class is the basis of British politics, all else is embellishment and detail'. At that time there was still a considerable degree of class alignment — a close correlation between an individual's social class and their natural party. This meant that those in social classes A, B and C1 tended to vote Conservative, whereas those in groups C2, D and E favoured Labour.

The 1970s and 1980s saw massive changes in the UK, both in terms of employment and in society as a whole. The result of these changes was a gradual process of embourgeoisement, where working-class people came to see themselves as middle class and voted accordingly. This led to theories of class dealignment, with the Conservatives under Margaret Thatcher able to win elections by reaching out to the C2s. Although the strong correlation that once existed between social class and voting has clearly declined over time, it still remains an important influence. For example, in 2005 only 28% of those in classes A and B voted Labour compared to 48% of those in classes D and E.

There are other long-term influences on voting behaviour apart from social class. Older voters are said to be more likely to vote Conservative than Labour. Gender has also been a factor in the past, with women more likely to vote Conservative and men more likely to vote Labour. In part this gender gap reflected the historic links between the Labour Party and male union members working in heavy industry, allied to the traditional (conservative) roles that many women played in the home. The decline of heavy industry and union membership, coupled with the modern tendency for women to go out to work, has weakened such ties — as have Labour's efforts to court the female vote.

As a result, short-term factors are now far more important than long-term factors in determining the outcome of general elections. Such short-term factors include issues, the relative merits of the party leaders and the campaign itself.

Sorry, ran out of time.

Although this candidate ran out of time, having spent rather too long on part (b), there is still a good deal to recommend this response. The effective use of political vocabulary (e.g. embourgeoisement, class dealignment, gender gap) would all be worthy of credit on AO3. This answer is also strong in terms of focus and argument/analysis (AO2). It is a pity that a lack of time prevented the candidate from developing some of the references to short-term factors made in the closing paragraph, but there is probably still enough here for a mark equivalent to a **bottom A grade**.

C-grade answer

(a) Opinion polls are a 'snap-shot' of public opinion, of how people may vote. But they are not always reliable. In 1992 the polls were 9% out. This may have been because people lied to pollsters. Politicians say that they don't listen to bad poll ratings, but they can be damaging, e.g. Thatcher in 1990 and Blair after Iraq.

The candidate offers a fairly limited definition and makes no explicit reference to the extract. That said, the reference to polling errors in 1992, and the explanation that follows, is worth of some credit. The answer would gain **a mid C grade**.

(b) Newspapers can have a massive impact on election campaigns. Unlike the coverage on television news, the press does not have to stay politically neutral. As a result, many newspapers give open backing to a particular party in the election. The *Sun* used to back Labour before Murdoch bought it and turned it into a Tory paper in the 1980s. Then it went back to Labour in 1997. This is really important. Millions of people read the *Sun* every day, or at least look at the pictures! Even if 1% of them are persuaded to vote a particular way then that could make a big difference in a marginal constituency. The anti-Labour headlines in the 1992 general election are mentioned in the extract and probably affected the result. In 1997 Blair did a deal with Murdoch. Blair promised to leave his media empire alone in return for Murdoch backing New Labour. It was all agreed on a trip to Australia. All of Murdoch's papers — the *Sun*, the *News of the World* and *The Times* — have backed Labour ever since. It can't be a coincidence that Labour started winning elections as soon as Murdoch got on board.

There is lots of good content here on newspaper campaigns (AO1), although this material is a little too descriptive (i.e. weaker on AO2). It is also rather narrow, referring only to newspapers when the question clearly states 'media'. It is a **mid C-grade** response.

(c) Debates concerning the main influences on voting behaviour normally revolve around whether or not short-term (or recency) factors are now more important than the long-term (or primacy) in deciding the outcome of general elections.

In the 1950s and 1960s long-term factors were certainly said to be crucial. Most people were said to vote on the basis of their social class, with working-class voters backing Labour and middle-class voters supporting the Tories. Things have changed however. Modern parties are less class-based and less ideological. They are now election-winning machines rather than mass member organisations. With so few fundamental differences between the parties, recency factors are now the key to success.

Issues matter. In every election there are three or four important issues. Political scientists call these the 'salient' issues, e.g. immigration, the state of the economy, interest rates. Some events are also shaped by a major crisis or controversy that emerges ahead of polling day, e.g. the Winter of Discontent in 1979, the Falklands factor in 1983, sleaze in 1997 or Iraq in 2005.

The image of the party leaders is also important. Although people are really voting for their own MP, they are less likely to vote for the candidate of a party led by someone who they do not see as prime ministerial material.

The candidate provides a fair overview of some of the main influences on voting behaviour, without really offering developed analysis on any single factor. At the very least, one would expect those answering this question to be able to offer something more on the strength of the correlation between social class and voting. Despite this, the response would still be pushing up towards the **B/C-grade boundary**.

Question 2

Electoral systems

Read the extract below and answer parts (a) to (c) which follow.

Single transferable vote

Single transferable vote (STV) is a proportional electoral system used in Northern Ireland (in assembly elections, local elections and elections to the European Parliament), as well as in Scottish local elections since 2007. Supporters of STV tend to focus on its perceived fairness, in particular the way in which the system virtually eliminates **wasted votes**.

STV operates using multi-member constituencies and a preferential voting system, where electors indicate their preferences by writing '1' beside the name of their first preference, '2' next to the name of their second choice and so on. Electors can vote for as many or as few candidates as they like. In order to win one of the seats available in a given multi-member constituency, a candidate must achieve a quota — a fixed number of the total number of valid votes cast. Any votes that a candidate secures in excess of this quota are redistributed on the basis of second preferences until no more quotas can be filled in this way. At that point, the lowest placed candidate would be eliminated and their votes transferred. This process of vote transference and elimination would take place until the number of candidates achieving the quota was equal to the number of seats available.

Source: adapted in part from Mark Garnett and Philip Lynch,
UK Government & Politics, Philip Allan Updates (2005).

(a) Explain the term 'wasted votes' used in the extract. (5 marks)

(b) Using your own knowledge as well as the extract, examine the likely consequences of the UK adopting the single transferable vote system (STV) for use in elections to the Westminster Parliament. (10 marks)

(c) 'Experiments in the use of a range of voting systems other than FPTP around the UK since 1997 have resulted in more harm than good.' Assess the accuracy of this view. (25 marks)

(a) When defining the term 'wasted votes' it is important to include the surplus votes secured by a winning candidate (i.e. the votes he or she did not need to win) as well as those cast in favour of all other candidates. The extract refers to the way in which STV should virtually eliminate wasted votes. The ability to offer an example of wasted votes from your own knowledge would make it more likely that you will achieve the higher levels on the mark scheme.

(b) Although this question is referring to the likely consequences of introducing STV in general elections, it is just as valid for you to base your analysis upon the actual impact of elections under STV in Northern Ireland as it is to argue entirely on the basis of a theoretical understanding of the mechanics of STV. Make sure that you deal with at least two or three separate consequences.

(c) In order to answer this question you will need to have a good understanding of how some or all of the various systems introduced since 1997 (i.e. party list, AMS, STV and SV) have affected electoral outcomes. You could focus your answer around factors such as proportionality, voter choice, the MP–constituency link, and the nature of the resulting government (majority or coalition).

■ ■ ■

A-grade answer

(a) The total number of wasted votes in a given constituency is calculated by subtracting the number of votes that the victorious candidate needed to win from the total number of votes that were cast in that election. First-past-the-post results in large numbers of wasted votes because a candidate need only secure one vote more than his/her nearest rival in order to win. With several candidates standing in each election this means that the winner will often secure a good deal fewer than 50% of the total votes cast. In St Albans in 2005 around 30,000 of the 45,000 votes cast were wasted. The extract says that STV 'virtually eliminates wasted votes'. This is because it uses a preferential voting system where votes that might otherwise be wasted are normally transferred until they count for someone.

> ✒ This is a really precise definition and demonstrates good knowledge, both to explain the term in the context of FPTP and to provide a specific example. The fact that the candidate also manages to link the discussion back to the extract (with the closing comments regarding STV) singles this out as a top level response. **Full marks**.

(b) A switch to using STV in UK general elections would bring a number of consequences for voters. We can already see what a difference STV has made in Northern Ireland. The likely consequences can be divided up into four main areas: voter choice; proportionality; the MP–constituency link; and the nature of government.

STV uses a preferential voting system alongside multi-member constituencies. This means that voters will have a lot more choice than is present under the current first-past-the-post system. Because each of the major parties will probably put up enough candidates to fill all of the seats available in the constituency, voters will be able to cast all of their preferences for candidates of their favoured party, or to share their preferences among other parties or independent candidates. It should mean that tactical voting, as we know it, will be a thing of the past. This is because voters will be able to put their favoured candidate at number '1', and then put their next best option as one of their preferences.

Because votes are transferred under STV, there will be far fewer wasted votes and the outcome should be more proportional in terms of votes won and seats won. In the 2003 elections to the Northern Ireland Assembly, Sinn Fein secured 23% of

question

first preference votes and ended up with 24% of seats. The SDLP got 17% of first preferences and 18% of seats. This greater proportionality would probably be repeated in UK general elections.

Because of bigger, multi-member constituencies, voters will effectively have more than one MP. This is bad in the sense that an individual voter will no longer have a single MP who is there to represent them. On the plus side, however, it makes it more likely that one of your MPs will be someone who you feel you can talk to. It is likely that STV would result in an increase in the number of women and ethnic minorities in Parliament, so that might also be a good thing.

STV tends to result in coalitions. This could be good or bad depending on how many parties are involved, i.e. how stable the coalition is.

The candidate provides an effective and clear analytical structure here, with four areas for discussion clearly identified at the outset. The balance between theory (the workings of STV) and examples (Northern Ireland) is particularly impressive. However, attempting to tackle four separate areas in answer to a part (b) question may be a little too ambitious. This candidate clearly runs out of time before he/she is able to deal effectively with the final point. It might be better to pick three areas and make sure that you cover these properly. Despite this, though, this response would still be regarded as a **top A-grade** answer.

(c) When New Labour came to power in 1997, all major elections in the UK took place under the simple plurality, first-past-the-post system. One of Labour's manifesto commitments in that general election had been a review into the use of this system in elections to the Westminster Parliament. Though the recommendations of this review, conducted by the Jenkins Commission, were not implemented, New Labour's first decade in power did see the introduction of a range of alternative systems in other elections around the UK.

One of Labour's first acts in government was to deliver on its manifesto commitment of creating a Scottish parliament and Welsh assembly. It was decided that these bodies would be elected under a variant of the AMS system known as first-past-the-post top-up. Most would argue that the Scottish experience under this system has been fairly favourable. First, it has extended voter choice, as Scots now have two votes in elections to the Scottish Parliament — one for their constituency MSP and one for their preferred party in the regional top-up contests. The system has also offered greater proportionality, with parties who had been disadvantaged under the FPTP system alone being rewarded under the top-up. Both the Conservatives and the SNP have benefited significantly in this way. For example, 13 of the Conservatives' 17 MSPs were elected from the top-up in 2007 compared to only nine of Labour's 46 MSPs returned. Though some were concerned that the system might create a kind of 'two-class' system of MSPs, some with constituencies and some without, this does not appear to have happened. Scotland has also faired reasonably well under coalition government (1999–2007) and minority government (after 2007). Indeed, some would argue that those north of the border have actually ended up with better policy than those in England and Wales, e.g. no top-up fees, free nursing care for the elderly, a better Freedom of Information Act etc.

Use of the closed regional list system in elections to the European Parliament could be said to have had more mixed results. Though the system has seen more parties winning seats (e.g. UKIP won 12 in 2004), the use of a regional, party-based system does not really allow for a strong MEP–constituency link. Use of the system has also failed to bring about the increase in turnout that had been hoped for at the time of its introduction.

The use of STV in Northern Ireland, and in Scottish local elections since 2007, has been fairly successful. Though few in Ireland appear to fully understand the workings of the system, it has contributed to more proportional outcomes, in the Northern Ireland Assembly at least. This is important in a region where people were often left feeling unrepresented and disengaged under FPTP. Though the Northern Ireland executive was operating under a DUP/Sinn Fein coalition in 2007, most appeared to view this as part of the success story in Northern Ireland — a sign of strength as opposed to weakness.

In conclusion, though Labour's experiments with a range of electoral systems have been rather piecemeal they have — by luck or by judgement — resulted in far more good than harm.

🖉 This candidate probably spends a little too long dealing with AMS, the result being that there is no time to mention SV — even in passing — and that the conclusion ends up being somewhat truncated. Despite this, the answer is focused and analytical throughout, ending with a judgement that is fully supported by the preceding discussion. **Top A grade.**

C-grade answer

(a) Systems such as first-past-the-post are not proportional. This means that there are a lot of wasted votes because some parties end up needing a lot more votes per seat won nationally. For example, in 2005 the Liberal Democrats averaged 97,000 votes per seat won, whereas Labour averaged 27,000. This means that lots of Liberal Democrat votes were wasted. All of the BNP's votes were wasted because they didn't win any seats.

🖉 The answer gives no real definition or explicit reference to the extract, but provides some excellent illustrative examples which suggest that the candidate understands the term. **Borderline B/C grade.**

(b) STV is a proportional system used in many elections in Northern Ireland. STV uses larger multi-member constituencies. Voters put down numbers to show their preferences. In order to be elected, a candidate must achieve the droop quota. Surplus votes are then transferred in accordance with second preferences. Where no candidate is elected on first preferences, the bottom candidate is knocked out and their votes are transferred. In the end all of the seats are filled.

Most voters don't understand how STV works. This could undermine confidence in the system, as could the fact that it may take a week to work out the result. STV has been good for Northern Ireland though. It has clearly resulted in more proportionality than FPTP — especially in the assembly elections.

By rewarding parties on both sides of the religious divide in Northern Ireland more fairly, the system has led to coalitions in the Northern Ireland executive. Although some thought that this might result in greater conflict, it has actually helped to enhance representation and reduce sectarianism, e.g. Ian Paisley (DUP) sitting down as first minister with Sinn Fein's Martin McGuinness as his deputy.

> ✏ There is a lot of good knowledge in the first paragraph but little analysis and no real focus on the precise terms of the question. The candidate provides a good deal more analysis in paragraphs 2 and 3, though again the focus is more on the actual outcomes under STV in Northern Ireland as opposed to the likely consequences for UK general elections. Though the candidate clearly knows his/her stuff, there would need to be at least some explicit focus on the question to take this beyond a C grade. **Low C grade.**

(c) In terms of proportionality, the systems introduced since 1997 have been a total success. The Scottish Socialists and the Greens have been able to win seats in the Scottish Parliament under AMS, and the Greens have also been able to take two seats in the European Parliament in 1999 and 2004 under party list. Outcomes under STV have also been more proportional.

Some would argue that coalition government in Scotland (1999–2007), in Wales for a time, and in Northern Ireland, has been a bad thing — but the people do not appear to have suffered a great deal under multi-party government. Indeed, Scottish students are probably better off as they don't have top-up fees up there.

One of the biggest problems with the new systems that Labour brought in after 1997 was that of representation. Scottish people now use a total of four separate electoral systems across various elections: FPTP in general elections; AMS in elections to the Scottish Parliament; party list in elections to the European Parliament; and STV in local elections. This has resulted in chaos — you only need to look at the 100,000 plus spoilt ballots in the 2007 Scottish Parliament elections.

The other problem is the West Lothian question. How can it be fair that Scottish MPs at Westminster can vote on laws that only affect voters in England and Wales? Why should we end up with top-up fees just because the support of Labour MPs representing Scottish constituencies carried the bill through Westminster? Worse still, why should English taxpayers continue to subsidise the Scots to the tune of £2,000 per head when they have their own parliament with tax-varying powers north of the border?

🖉 This answer is not bad at all on the consequences for Scotland but a good deal more limited on the impact of AMS elsewhere, and on the impact of other systems. The last paragraph drifts totally off-topic and, for that matter, off-unit. The West Lothian question has nothing to do with the use of AMS in elections to the Scottish Parliament. **Mid C grade**.

uestion 3

Political parties

Read the extract below and answer parts (a) to (c) which follow.

From Old Labour to New Labour

Michael Foot (Labour leader 1980–83) initially tried to sustain a compromise between Labour's socialist wing and the social democrats on the right of the party. The departure of four leading figures on the right to form the Social Democratic Party (SDP) in 1981 resulted in Labour moving sharply to the left. The party's manifesto in the 1983 general election — later dubbed 'the longest suicide note in history' — certainly played some part in bringing about a crushing victory for the Conservatives in that election.

After 1983 the new Labour Leader, Neil Kinnock, looked to root out those on the extreme left of the party, such as the Militant Tendency. Following further general election defeats in 1987 and 1992, Neil Kinnock's successor, John Smith, looked to continue the process of reform. Smith's sudden death in 1994 resulted in yet another Labour leadership election. The victor in this contest, Tony Blair, completed Labour's modernisation programme. He persuaded the party to drop its historic commitment to state ownership of key industries ('Clause IV') and rebranded the party as New Labour.

Source: adapted in part from Mark Garnett and Philip Lynch,
UK Government & Politics, Philip Allan Updates (2005).

(a) Explain the term 'Old Labour' used in the title of the extract. (5 marks)

(b) Using your own knowledge as well as the extract, examine two or more ways in which Tony Blair changed the Labour Party between 1994 and 2007. (10 marks)

(c) 'Power within modern UK political parties is held by the party leaders and other senior figures as opposed to individual members.' Discuss. (25 marks)

(a) The extract focuses on Labour's transformation between the party's landslide defeat in the 1983 general election and Tony Blair's historic move to drop the old Clause IV in 1995. In detailing the emergence of New Labour, the extract also identifies a number of features commonly associated with 'Old Labour' (e.g. a commitment to socialism, state ownership of key industries etc.). You should bring in your own knowledge too, perhaps by referring to Labour's traditional core support or the party's origins in the unions and socialist societies of the late nineteenth and early twentieth centuries.

(b) The extract uses the word 'modernisation', in reference to Labour's abandonment of Clause IV and its 'rebranding' as New Labour. Your own knowledge could be used either to develop these points or to identify and discuss other aspects of

Labour's transformation, e.g. specific changes in policy, the use of all-women shortlists, media management and the emphasis on style/presentation ('spin'). Remember to develop at least two areas fully.

(c) This question is clearly focused on the issue of internal party democracy. Try to divide your discussion between areas such as control over policy formation and candidate selection. Remember, although your focus is likely to be on the two main UK parties, relevant and accurate references to where power lies within the Liberal Democrats will also be credited fully.

■ ■ ■

A-grade answer

(a) The Labour Party emerged from the trade union movement and socialist societies of the late nineteenth century. It was created to represent the needs of the working classes. Clause IV of the party's 1918 constitution offered a clear commitment to socialism. This is what Old Labour was all about. The extract talks about the party's commitment to 'state ownership of key industries'. Old Labour was also committed to progressive taxation and the welfare state. This is why it was the party of choice for what Ivor Crewe called the 'old working class'. But the country changed in the 1970s and 1980s and Blair was forced to abandon a lot of this in order to be elected — hence New Labour.

> 🖉 The candidate gives a clear link to the extract (state ownership), some of their own knowledge (progressive taxation), and a clear definition, although it is rather too narrative in style. **Mid A grade.**

(b) Tony Blair oversaw a massive programme of Labour Party modernisation between 1994, when he was elected party leader, and the handover to Gordon Brown in 2007. This modernisation can be broadly divided into three main areas: party organisation; party policy; and party image.

Blair made a number of significant changes to the way in which the party was organised. First, he carried on and completed the work which Kinnock and Smith had started in moving the party away from its reliance on the unions. The block vote was limited with the extension of one-member-one-vote (OMOV) into many areas of party organisation. Blair also reorganised the way in which the party made policy, introducing a 2-year cycle and thereby reducing the power of the annual conference.

In terms of policy, the party under Blair was unrecognisable from that which had gone into the 1983 general election under Michael Foot. Under Blair the party accepted the basic principles of 'the market', adopted the previous Conservative government's plans on tax and spending and refused to undo the anti-union legislation passed under Thatcher in the 1980s. Blair also tried to close the gender gap by making the party more women-friendly. Labour used all-women shortlists in many safe seats and also offered help with childcare, e.g. money to pay for nurseries.

The final and maybe the biggest area of change was in image. Old Labour became New Labour. Leading Labour MPs lost their beards and gained sharp suits and pagers. Alastair Campbell kept everyone 'on message', through the Milbank media and communications centre, as the emphasis moved from policy detail to presentation. Some didn't like this 'spin', but it all helped to make the party electable.

> ✐ This is a good answer in terms of overall length, structure and focus. Some sections are a little too casual ('Labour MPs lost their beards and gained sharp suits and pagers'), but this does not detract from the overall quality. There is excellent use of examples. **Top A grade.**

(c) This question is clearly focusing on the issue of internal party democracy — that is, where precisely power rests within the main UK parties: with grassroots members, or with the party leaders.

In terms of making party policy, it is probably fair to say that ultimate power now tends to rest with those who lead the parties. After all, it would be hard for a party to require its leaders to head up policies which they themselves didn't believe in. In the Conservative Party the leader has always had the key role in formulating policy, though he or she is expected to take on board the views of others, e.g. the front bench, the 1922 Committee, party elders, and the grassroots membership. In the 1990s, William Hague sought to democratise the party's policy-making process with his 'Fresh Future' initiative. Even so, the bodies he created — the National Conservative Convention and the Conservative Political Forum — were little more than advisory. Under Blair the Labour Party has also seen a shift in policy-making power to the centre. In the 1970s 'the conference was king' in terms of deciding policy. Under Blair, however, the party adopted a 2-year policy-making cycle, with the National Policy Forum appointing policy commissions that make proposals which are then formalised in the National Executive Committee (NEC) before being passed to the party conference for final approval. These new arrangements helped to avoid the bitter arguments and 'Micky Mouse' policies that characterised the old-style conferences, such as that in 1983.

In terms of selecting parliamentary candidates, all three major UK parties follow a similar three-stage process: first, those wanting to be candidates must get themselves onto a centrally vetted list of approved candidates; second, they must be shortlisted by the constituency party; and third, they must be chosen by local members, either at a constituency meeting (for the Conservatives) or by secret ballot. Even then, however, the central party can still step in by rejecting the local candidate and imposing its own, e.g. Labour's imposition of former Conservative MP Shaun Woodward in St Helens.

All three major parties give individual members a say in choosing their party leader. Liberal Democrat members get a chance to vote by secret ballot once the candidates have been officially nominated. Following the reforms put in place by William Hague, individual Conservative Party members also get a vote, once MPs have whittled the field down to two candidates. The only problem with the

Conservative system is that MPs can manipulate the choice given to members in such a way as to get the result they want or, as was the case with Michael Howard's coronation, only put up a single candidate, thus removing the right of members to vote at all. The Labour Party did something similar when choosing Gordon Brown as its leader without opposition. Normally, Labour members would form one third of the Electoral College that chooses between the available candidates.

In a sense one could argue that internal democracy is probably not a good idea anyway. When party membership was far higher, the views of members may well have offered a fair reflection of the views of the broader public. In the modern era, however, members are often entirely unrepresentative of the population at large. Allowing individual members too much power could therefore amount to electoral suicide.

🖉 Although this candidate writes a good deal more than most others would be able to do in the time available, they largely manage to avoid irrelevance. That said, although the penultimate paragraph would be good in answer to a general question on internal party democracy, one could question whether or not the candidate really does enough here to link it to the question posed. The final paragraph makes an excellent analytical point (AO2). **Top A grade.**

C-grade answer

(a) Old Labour is the opposite of New Labour. Blair abandoned Clause IV and tried to make Labour more like the Conservatives, e.g. by accepting Thatcherism and going for middle England. This is all part of the 'end of ideology'. It is true that all of the major parties are the same nowadays. Maybe this is because everyone thinks that they are middle class so we don't need a working-class party like Old Labour was. If people want something like Old Labour then they have to vote for the Scottish Socialists or Socialist Labour.

🖉 This candidate demonstrates a reasonable understanding of the term, but without ever offering a clear definition or exposition of what 'Old Labour' stood for. Ideally, they would also have made explicit reference to the material provided in the extract. **Mid C grade.**

(b) Tony Blair transformed the Labour Party between 1994 and 2007. As the extract says, the first thing that he did was to dump Clause IV. This clause had committed the Labour Party to state ownership of key industries, so getting rid of it meant that they were willing to have privatisation.

Blair also changed the style of the Labour Party. Before Blair, the party had been all about the unions. It was seen as the party of unionised working-class men and it didn't really appeal to the middle classes or to women. This may be why women used to vote more for the Conservatives. Blair changed all of that. Labour tidied up its image, got a new logo (the red rose) and started calling itself New Labour. Blair

---

himself was a different kind of leader — more of a typical Conservative leader really. He was a public-school and Oxford-educated lawyer. This made it easier for him to take the party in a new direction. He was good with sound-bites and he also looked good on camera, at least better than the four previous Labour leaders.

> The first paragraph is relevant but it doesn't really do anything more than restate what is said in the extract. The second paragraph is far more impressive: the candidate moves beyond the extract and makes one or two good individual points on the theme of Blair's impact on the style/image of the party. This level of development needed to be applied to other areas too (e.g. Labour policy) in order for the answer to score more highly overall. As it is, this is rather too narrow. **Mid C grade**.

(c) The Liberal Democrats are by far the most internally democratic of the three main UK political parties. The party has a federal structure, with English, Scottish and Welsh state parties, below which are a further four, three, and three tiers respectively. Decisions are taken at the most appropriate level, i.e. this is called subsidiarity. The bi-annual federal conference is the supreme policy-making body in the party. It deals with policy proposals from the Federal Policy Committee, state, regional and local parties.

The party leadership has a good deal of control over the Federal Policy Committee, so the party's leaders can normally manage to avoid being saddled with policies that make the party unelectable. Despite this, it is argued that some of the party's policies in the 2005 general election (e.g. on cannabis possession, asylum seekers and local income tax) were rather too easily attacked by Labour and the Conservatives. In this sense, one of the party's strengths (its internal democracy) might also be its greatest weakness.

When choosing their party leaders, the Liberal Democrats are also the most democratic of the three main parties. Liberal Democrat leadership elections operate under an STV system using one member one vote (OMOV). Those wishing to stand must be proposed and seconded by fellow MPs and nominated by no fewer than 200 members from at least 20 different local parties.

Compared to the Liberal Democrats, both Labour and the Conservatives appear rather top-down in terms of power. Under Blair, power became far more concentrated around the party leader and his senior allies in Parliament. The Conservative leader has always had virtual carte blanche when deciding major issues of party policy.

> Though this candidate is able to demonstrate a good level of knowledge and understanding relating to the Liberal Democrats, the focus of the answer is far too narrow. Even if a candidate's knowledge is more developed in one area than another, they will still be expected to make more than passing reference to other areas as a means of providing context and balance. Though the candidate does this in the final paragraph, the focus of this answer is still too narrow overall. **Mid C grade**.

90

Pressure groups and protest movements

Read the extract below and answer parts (a) to (c) which follow.

Pressure group typologies

The diversity and sheer number of pressure groups has made generalisation and categorisation difficult for political scientists. One of the earliest attempts was made by J. D. Stewart, who distinguished between sectional groups and **cause groups**. Wyn Grant has made a different distinction, that between 'insider' and 'outsider' groups. He focuses on their relationship to central decision-makers, i.e. a group's 'status'. Some critics of Grant's model argue that he overstates the difficulty of achieving insider status. Others note that groups may pursue insider and outsider strategies simultaneously or that groups can move in and out of favour very quickly. This need for greater precision has led Grant and others to advance a number of sub-categories, e.g. core insiders, specialist insiders, and peripheral insiders.

Source: adapted from Christopher Wilson, *AS-Level Government and Politics*,
Manchester University Press (2003).

(a) Explain the term 'cause groups' used in the extract. (5 marks)

(b) Using your own knowledge as well as the extract, identify and explain two or more criticisms of the insider/outsider typology. (10 marks)

**(c) 'Pressure group success is largely dependent upon group resources.'
To what extent would you agree with this view?** (25 marks)

    (a) The extract identifies cause groups as one half of a pressure group typology originally developed by J. D. Stewart. It then contrasts this method of categorising pressure groups with the insider/outsider typology developed by Wyn Grant and others. You could use your own knowledge to provide examples of cause groups or to demonstrate a greater understanding of the model, perhaps by referring to sub-categories, e.g. attitude cause groups.

    (b) The material provided identifies three distinct problems with the insider/outsider typology: first, that it is easier than one might think to obtain insider status; second, that a group's status can change quickly between insider and outsider; and third, that many groups appear to be in both 'camps' simultaneously. You could use your own knowledge to provide examples (e.g. the changing fortunes of the National Farmers Union) or to show the need for greater precision (e.g. core insiders, potential insiders etc.).

    (c) Avoid focusing entirely on group resources when answering this question. You should instead aim to put resources into context alongside other factors that can affect group success, e.g. group aims, group methods and group status. Ideally, you should also demonstrate how some or all of these factors are linked, e.g. that a group's methodology is likely to be shaped by the presence or absence of certain resources, or the extent to which the government is receptive to that group's stated aims.

■ ■ ■

A-grade answer

(a) Cause groups are one half of the cause/sectional group typology. As the extract says, this was one of the earliest attempts to classify pressure groups. This typology divides groups according to their aims, rather than their status in relation to government. Cause groups, sometimes called promotional groups, can be further sub-divided into those that represent a particular group of society (sectional cause groups such as Shelter), those that try to change attitudes in a particular area of policy (attitude cause groups such as Greenpeace) and those that look to secure a set of clearly defined political objectives (political cause groups such as Charter 88). One of the problems with this typology is that groups can often be said to fit into more than one box.

> This candidate clearly understands the term on a theoretical level and also recognises that the typology is less than perfect in practice. The awareness of sub-categories and examples demonstrated here would all be credited fully. **High A grade**.

(b) The extract identifies a number of problems with Wyn Grant's insider/outsider typology, but there are others too. The first point made in the extract is that it really isn't that hard for groups to gain insider status. The whole point of Grant's typology is that access to inner government circles is restricted and limited, meaning that only a small number of well established and respected groups can be inside at any one time. In fact the situation is far more complicated. First, some groups can be insiders when certain issues are decided, but not at other times. Core insiders such as the RSPCA or the CBI may be consulted across a wide range of government policy, but other groups, called specialist insiders, may only seek or be granted insider status in their particular area of expertise.

The second problem with the typology is that group status can change very rapidly as a result of external events or following a change in government, e.g. when the Conservatives are in government the NFU has more access than under Labour, and vice versa with the trade unions.

Another point, which is not mentioned in the extract, is that some groups do not seek insider status, yet are still successful. Hunt saboteurs and groups campaigning against vivisection have clearly made an impact in recent years, yet neither have been welcomed with open arms by the government. Similarly, ideological outsiders such as Amnesty International, who avoid close contact with government as part of their desire to maintain their independence and impartiality, can still achieve a great deal.

In the past it was often said that outsider groups had to use high-profile stunts and direct action because they didn't have the government's ear. Now many groups are taking a positive decision to use such outsider tactics from the start, because direct action appears to offer a more direct route to success.

☑ The candidate makes good use of the extract and their own knowledge in order to make a number of valid points. The final two paragraphs of the answer demonstrate particularly high levels of analysis and evaluation (AO2). There is good theoretical awareness and excellent examples throughout. **High A grade.**

(c) The resources available to a group will play a key part in determining that group's chances of achieving its goals. Though the aims of a given group, the methods it adopts and its status in relation to the government will also be important, a pressure group will achieve little unless it has access to the necessary resources.

In the context of pressure group activity, resources can be broadly divided into human resources and material resources. Successful groups often have well developed human resources. This can mean having large numbers of members. Groups with large memberships often have access to better revenue streams and they also benefit from the greater legitimacy that having a large individual membership can afford a group, e.g. Greenpeace. Government is more likely to listen to broad-based groups. Human resources might also refer to the extent to which a given group has the skills that it needs from within its core membership, as opposed to having to buy in expertise. Groups whose members are educated and articulate are more likely to succeed, as are groups that have the necessary legal advice and PR skills immediately on tap. Groups without good human resources can still thrive where material resources (e.g. finances, facilities, equipment) are readily available, e.g. non-membership business groups. Groups with poor human resources and limited material resources are unlikely to be able to take full advantage of the access points available to them.

Aside from group resources, group aims are also crucial in determining a pressure group's chances of success. A group with aims that are readily achievable (e.g. stopping a single construction project) are far more likely to succeed than those campaigning against globalisation. How receptive the general public is to a group's aims can also prove crucial — and this can change over time.

The methods or tactics that a group adopts will clearly play a part in determining its chances of success. The most successful groups often adopt a range of strategies, with some designed to bring short-term benefits and some more focused on the long-term. Fathers4Justice, for example, didn't just dress up as superheroes and climb up public buildings — they also had a media strategy in place to deal with the phone calls and requests for television interviews that invariably came in the wake of their stunts.

The status afforded to a group by the government of the day will also affect that group's chances. Groups given high levels of access to the machinery of government may exert great influence, even where their media footprint is negligible. Groups that take positions which are diametrically opposed to the government of the day are likely to find their way blocked at every turn.

In conclusion, group success is clearly dependent on a range of interconnected and overlapping factors.

> 🖉 This response is strong on the theoretical importance of group resources, though a greater willingness/ability to use examples would take the answer to higher levels on AO2. The candidate successfully puts the importance of resources into context alongside other factors. The conclusion lacks development, but this is still a **mid A-grade** response.

C-grade answer

(a) Cause groups campaign for a particular cause (e.g. Greenpeace). Sectional groups look to protect the interests of a particular section of society (e.g. the British Medical Association). In recent years there has been a rise in single-issue cause groups. Such groups, like animal rights groups, often use direct action and sometimes even break the law. One group even dug up someone's mother-in-law in order to try to get a guinea pig farm shut down. This makes them more of a terrorist group really.

> 🖉 This answer starts off well but then gets sidetracked by a discussion of single-issue groups. It is crucial that you answer this year's paper, as opposed to a similar part (a) question that may have turned up in previous years. **Mid C grade.**

(b) The insider/outsider typology is a way of classifying pressure groups by their status in relation to decision-makers as opposed to their aims. Insider groups have greater access to government and are therefore more likely to achieve their goals. Insider status normally goes to established groups that have something to offer the government (e.g. expertise) or big groups that the government may want to get on board as a way of adding a degree of legitimacy to government decision-making. Insider groups can be sub-divided into core insiders (e.g. the BMA), specialist insiders (e.g. RoSPA) and peripheral insiders (e.g. the Canine Defence League). Outsiders can be divided into potential insiders, outsiders by necessity and ideological outsiders (e.g. Amnesty International).

Outsider groups tend to use more direct public protests because they are not invited into private consultation with the government. Insider groups do not use such direct tactics. For one thing, they don't need to — as the government is talking to them in secret anyway. For another, the government would take away their insider status if groups organised embarrassing publicity campaigns. It isn't the done thing for an insider group to embarrass the government.

Just because a group is an outsider does not mean that it will fail. Some insider groups probably have less influence than some big, effective outsider groups. After all, no one really listened to those campaigning for the rights of fathers until the group Fathers4Justice started dressing up as Spider-Man and climbed up parliament.

> ✏ Does this really answer the question posed? The opening paragraph, though sound in terms of factual knowledge, has little to do with criticisms of the insider/outsider typology. The same could also be said of the second paragraph, though it does at least provide some analysis. This would be a difficult answer to mark. On the one hand, there is plenty of good, accurate factual knowledge here. On the other, the fact that there is no real attempt to address the question means that this response is very limited on AO2. **D/C grade borderline**.

(c) The question is right to say that pressure group success is largely dependent upon group resources. This is because without resources, none of the other factors that are in the mix really matter that much.

Human resources are crucial to any group's chances of success. The media has become increasingly important in recent years and groups whose leading members are good in front of a camera or on the radio are therefore much more likely to make the right kind of impact. Though media skills can be bought in (if the group has good financial resources), people with these kinds of skills do not come cheap. Fathers4Justice benefited from the fact that their 'leader' had worked in marketing. While others scaled the Palace of Westminster, he was in the studio explaining the message behind the stunts. Other groups have members or supporters with good legal skills. This is particularly important if the group in question wishes to use legal action as one of its key tactics, e.g. Surfers Against Sewage or the Pro-Life Alliance.

Material resources are also important to any group. Though in the IT-age groups no longer need their own printing presses, they still require access to office space, telephone lines and — increasingly — the equipment necessary to maintain their own websites and manage online credit-card donations. It would be hard to manage a modern nationwide pressure group without a permanent base, secretarial support, and a convincing presence on the web — although some rely almost entirely on the internet.

Within the broad category of material resources, financial resources are clearly crucial to group success. Groups such as Greenpeace are able to conduct massive operations around the world simply because it has the equipment in storage, ready for use. In the case of the Brent Spar campaign, for example, Greenpeace was able to send out boats, climbing equipment and satellite broadcast systems to a location many miles off the coast of Scotland. Such an operation would be well beyond the capabilities of most groups as they simply wouldn't be able to afford to maintain such a stock of equipment. Other groups, such as Barnado's and the NSPCC, are able to buy up airtime and run advertisements on commercial television, resulting in further donations.

It is clear, therefore, that the resources available to a group will be crucial to its chances of success. Though other factors may also be significant (e.g. a group's aims), resources are the key to everything.

Though this answer is excellent on the importance of group resources, rather more is needed in terms of breadth. What about group aims, methodology or status? This failure to see the bigger picture would probably limit the response to a mark equivalent to a **top C grade**.